British Sport

A Social History

British Sport

A Social History

Dennis Brailsford

The Lutterworth Press

Cambridge

The Lutterworth Press
P.O. Box 60
Cambridge
CB1 2NT

British Library Cataloguing in Publication Data:
A catalogue record is available from the British Library.

ISBN 0 7188 2977 8

First published in hardback in the UK 1992
Revised paperback edition 1997

Printed in Great Britain by
Biddles Ltd, Kings Lynn, Norfolk

For Heather, Judith, and Robert.

Contents

Acknowledgements

My thanks are due to the University of Birmingham for continuing assistance from many quarters, from the University Library and from my colleagues in the School of Sport and Exercise Sciences, who continue to endure someone committed to the humanities.

Local sources such as the Dorset County Library and the Dorset County Museum have also contributed significantly, as has the ProFoLab, Weymouth, whose technical expertise has often worked wonders with inexpert photography.

I am grateful to the City of Dundee Art Galleries and Museums for permission to reproduce the Duncan Carse painting, *The Village Ba' Game*, and to Macmillan Publishing Company for permission to reproduce three prints from Cassell's *Illustrated History of England*.

Most of all, though, I am indebted to my research assistant, photographic adviser, proofreader, and patient travelling companion, namely my wife, whose endurance is matched only by her down-to-earth, good-humoured encouragement.

Illustrations

Chapter 5

Chapter 6

Chapter 7

Preface

British Sport
A Social History

This book tells the story of British sport, a continuing story from the Middle Ages to the present. Its aim is to give an overview of the styles of play that have marked the varying stages of British social history, and to show how these have fed into our contemporary experience.

The relevance of the organised and increasingly commercialised sport of the last hundred years is widely recognised, and dominates most histories. While its significance is acknowledged, this post-industrial history is only part of the story, and here it has to share the limelight. If it should be thought that justice is not fully done to the twentieth century, there is a wealth of other literature to make up any deficiency. Yet much of the play of the more distant past still has a recognisable relationship with our present-day sports. Bowls, archery, horse-racing, wrestling, athletics and cricket, as well as hunting and fishing, are among the many activities which would be familiar to a resurrected ancestor from long ago. Their meaning, their social significance, may have changed dramatically over the centuries - and this is one of the themes of this study - but this should not rule them out of consideration.

Quite apart from their contribution to our present lives, the sports of the past have left many marks on our physical environment, and these have largely gone unremarked. With this in mind, much of the illustration in this book is of existing sporting reminders of the past. Such signs lie all around us, and one of the hopes is that readers will be encouraged to look, to photograph, and to record. To demonstrate the local possibilities, many of the photographs here are from a single area, and one not particularly noteworthy in conventional sporting terms.

The social history of sport is still a young study, with many blank pages to be filled. Some ways in which this might be done are indicated in the last section of each chapter, where there are also some highly selective suggestions for further reading that could be helpful. The concentration here has been on accessibility, both in the physical sense of likely availability, and on readability. It has meant the exclusion of numerous worthwhile contributions to the study, and also, for instance of works such as William J. Baker's *Sports in the Western World* (Totawa, New Jersey, 1982), one of the very few quality histories to cover the whole historical span, but published only in North America.

The approach of the book is chronological, as befits a developing story. A broad survey of half a dozen centuries has, of necessity, to concentrate on selected topics within each period, and then to condense in their treatment. There is no space for a compendium of Derby winners or a list of Wimbledon champions, and it is no part of its intentions to provide such catalogues. Nor can it do justice to all the outstanding players and all the individual sports that have contributed to the fascinating history of play. Moreover, there is always some risk in claiming to present a history of *British* sport when so much of the account inevitably concentrates specifically on England, and on south-eastern England at that. Readers in other parts of these islands have a particular task in helping to fill the many persisting gaps in our public knowledge.

The hope of any writer who reflects on the lives of our forebears must be to bring them alive, to combine enlightenment with pleasure. This is all the more important when the central topic is sport and play, whose overwhelming features have to be the zest that inspires and the satisfaction that results. If we cannot play or watch all the time, there remains the alternative pleasure of finding out more about it, and even making our own discoveries from what lies to hand.

1

Let's Sport and Play

Whatever later lyricists may have made of some lost pastoral idyll, the truth is that we know far too little of the sports of our distant ancestors. Medieval writers have left only scant and scattered evidence of the people's play. Most were churchmen and latinists, and what went on in the churchyard or the village fields concerned them only if it affected the interests of the church or their lay patrons. Most of our written hints on the nature of sport, before the flowering of the English literature in the vernacular in the sixteenth century, come from such miscellaneous sources as sermons, court proceedings, ecclesiastical records, a few moral tales, and edicts to control or limit games.

Fortunately, the written word is not the only evidence. There is enough pictorial record to give some insights into how our forebears played, there is enduring corroboration in place-names and field names, for instance, and there are remnants of medieval rites and festivals that survived long enough to be recorded by eighteenth-century antiquarians, some even persisting until today. These latter, however, have to be treated with some caution. So-called 'revivals' of 'the past' have never been more prolific than in the theme-park Britain of the late twentieth century, when 'heritage' has become a national growth industry. Even the many festivals with a respectable ancestry have often had their interruptions, some for many years, and there can be no complete assurance that their present forms bear more than a vestigial resemblance to the original celebrations. Celebrations they were though, and in them were nurtured the distant seeds of our modern sport.

Rites and Revels
The earliest stages of sport - its anthropology - lie outside the scope of this book. An instinctive urge to run, to race, to throw, to dance, and to compete, is taken for granted, particularly among the young, and it is important to remember that in those distant days of short lives most populations were young. Pre-Christian rituals often formalised competitive behaviour into the physical expression of rivalry for the aid of magical forces. Out of this ritualistic play emerged habits of competition which eventually expanded beyond the contexts in which they had developed. Even primitive hunting, essential as it was for food and survival, was, it now seems, often pursued for fun as well as for nurture.

A handful of these competitive rites have still survived in communal 'football' games. In spite of being very widely spread, from the northernmost parts of the islands down to Cornwall, they have many features in common, pointing to a shared ancestry. For instance, both the Kirkwall football game from the Orkneys and the Haxey Hood game from Lincolnshire look much the same, with their massive scrums struggling to carry the ball to a home base, and both were given latter day explanations to mask their original significance. This was doubtless the conflict over an animal or even human head, whose blood would be held to make fruitful the fields of the victors - or, in the case of the 'Downies' at Kirkwall, who dip the ball in the harbour if they win, to prosper their fishing. The medieval account of the origins of the Lincolnshire game had the local lady of the manor lose her hood on a windy day and rewarding the peasants who rescued it with the use of the land where the event took place. The Orkney explication is less sanitised, and has a local hero racing after a fleeing tyrant as far south as Perth, where he killed him and brought his head back to the island, where it was competed over as a trophy.

It has become fashionable among sport historians to deny any meaningful connection between these ancient contests and modern sporting competition. Certainly so much is apparently different - the accidental inequality of numbers, the absence of either rules or a defined, playing area, the blurring of the distinction between players and spectators - that it is tempting to resist all identification of the old with the new. Yet the primeval passions of the local struggle, the communal collectivity of the teams and the crowds, the opportunity for the release of otherwise inhibited violence, these surely still have their echoes. Nor were the old games completely random. They had their set days as annual fixtures. The Haxey *boggons*, the official overseers, have to keep the struggle in the designated field as long as they can, and one account of the game speaks of rudimentary restraints, such as the caution that

'If tho' meets a man, knock 'im doone

But don't 'ut him.'

And as to the diversity of practices in these local games, another sign of their rudimentary nature, this itself is now repeated on the world scale. Football now takes in the global villages - three codes in Britain, four in Australia, and distinctive versions in, for instance, Ireland and North America, where the gridiron game even subdivides into United States and Canadian versions.

This is not to deny that the games of our ancestors were far removed from most of our present sporting activities. Their lives as a whole were so different that they had to be. Opportunities for leisure were limited by the unremitting demands of survival in a hard world. Play on any scale had to be occasional. There was no time to develop sophisticated games skills, nor indeed was there probably the energy, given nutritional levels, to indulge regularly in violent exercise for reasons other than sustenance. Game forms had to be simple enough to be passed on by imitation and word of mouth.

Originally, one of the more formal aspects of these communal games lay in their timing, their association with some particular calendar event, and a feature of the growth of sport in the Middle Ages was its gradual freeing from total dependence on set points in the ecclesiastical or agricultural year. Under the old pattern of celebration, each season had its own styles of play, many of them pre-Christian in origin but most adapted and tolerated, if not always encouraged, by the church. Some vestiges of that ancient rhythm of play are still with us, not only in the broad division between summer and winter sports but also in, for instance, the flurry of race meetings on Boxing Day and at Easter. They are, though, fading rapidly with the internationalisation of sport and the release of play from many of the old climatic restraints through floodlights, artificial turf, and covered domes.

The medieval sporting year began with the spring fertility festivals, some as early as Plough Monday just after Christmas (the occasion for the Haxey Hood game) but the majority focused on Eastertide, the first major occasion for sustained outdoor revelry. Shrove Tuesday became the last chance to let off the pent-up steam of winter before the denials of Lent, and its sports tended to be violent and combative - wrestling, tug o' war contests, animal baiting and fighting, skittles and bowls, as well as football. Cock-throwing was not completely put down as a Shrove Tuesday entertainment until well into the eighteenth-century - the bird was either tethered or perched on, or even in, a large earthenware pitcher, and then pelted with missiles until it broke free, was caught, and killed. It was excused as a symbolic assault on Pontius Pilate, represented by the cockerel, and, like many medieval sports had many local variants and almost as many names - *cock-squailing* (squailes were heavy sticks) and, in Devon, *cock-kibbit* are just two of them. To include bowls among the more boisterous games of Eastertide might seem surprising to an age used to the serene calm of the modern green, but it did not become a sport for those seeking peace and quiet until the last century, and again it embodied a whole range of games involving various forms of missiles and skittles. One Scots legend has it that the game originated when warriors played with the skulls of beaten enemies, a tale not entirely at odds with its long subsequent reputation for sharp practice, rowdiness, and even violence.

The summer games tended to be gentler. Running, jumping, and throwing contests came into their own. May Day, often marked by games in which young men chased young women (and the fertility rites became more than merely symbolic) and then Midsummer's Day were the original great playtimes of the summer. They gradually gave way to Whitsuntide, itself a pre-Christian festival eventually appropriated by the church. Whitsuntide was to become the high point of the sporting year, a time for dancing and country games, for barley break (another chasing game), for simple ball games, throwing and catching, for hitting balls with sticks, and above all for running races and for jumping contests. Ascension Day, which fell variably in early May according to the date of Easter, also came to have its importance in the embryonic sporting calendar and provides an interesting sidelight on one of the many ways in which more formal sports may have developed. It was the customary occasion in many places for beating the bounds of the parish, essential for confirming knowledge of boundaries and passing it on from one generation to the next. During the day-long perambulation the older men would encourage the youngsters to jump this ditch, race along this hedge, or climb this or that landmark, an event recalled by the Dorset poet, William Barnes, in early Victorian times. It is easy to imagine that such competitive feats, in the dim past, would encourage similar contests away from formal occasions.

Apart from this gradual breaking out of sport from the confines of the traditional calendar there was the growth of more distinctive games, some

A Victorian recreation of the amusements of the tiltyard, from Cassell's *History of England*.

of them recognisable as the direct ancestors of today's play. The process was already well under way by the end of the twelfth century. London might still have only some 20,000 souls but it was already urbanised enough to need some organisation in its play and was assuming the leading role in the development of sport that it was to hold until the Industrial Revolution. Football still seems to have been occasional, largely confined to Shrovetide, but as a boys' game there are hints of systematisation, some schools having their own 'teams,' which also played a stick and ball game, a likely ancestor of hockey. Shrovetide cock-fighting was another schoolboy sport, often supervised by the master - it was to remain so in some places, such as Wimborne Grammar School in Dorset, for over five centuries. Young men, presumably the more well-to-do among them, set up horse-races. There was jousting with blunted lances, and - for the more plebeian - tilting at the quintain, a target board hung at head height. For greater risk, and amusement, there was also a water-borne version where the target was attacked from a punt floated down on the tide and failure to strike it lunged the player into the river. Our leading contemporary authority on London sports at the end of the twelfth century, William Fitzstephen, tells us that 'all the Summer the youths are exercised in leaping, dancing, shooting, wrestling, casting the stone, and practising their shields,' while on winter afternoons there was boar-fighting and bull- and bear-baiting. When the marshes round the city were frozen over there was skating, using mutton shoulder-blade bones as skates and sometimes using a stick for propulsion, punting fashion.

That all these sports were still usually mentioned in association with holy days was inevitable. The holidays were the only times when people were free from work, but they were plentiful. Apart from the weekly holy day, usually observed from Saturday afternoon, there were at least thirty others that brought full- or half-day breaks. Most came between spring and autumn and sports ceased, for the most part, to be confined to some specific single festival - they were played on *all* the holy days in their season. There is, too, the first

Water-borne jousting, from one of the medieval woodcuts used by Joseph Strutt in his *Sport and Pastimes of the People of England* (1801).

evidence of spectators deliberately making their way to the sporting grounds, the richer and older men on horseback, to watch the contests oof the young.

Recognisable games were appearing. Corts, kails, hurling loggats, and hurling, for instance, were the likely ancestors of quoits, skittles, putting the shot, and a style of football. Their significance lies in their virtually complete separation from any ritualistic connotation, being played as games for their own sakes, with wagers already giving many of them an added spice. Meanwhile, on the broader political stage, a new sense of nationhood was emerging and the beginnings of national games were a minor sub-theme in the process of change. The Plantagenet kings were about to give up the half-completed task of uniting the British Isles and to embark on the Hundred Years War with France. At Crecy, in 1346, the new long-bows of the English would rain down their hail of arrows to great effect on the French. As they did so, they not only initiated a new phase in the history of warfare but also, in one sense, a new episode in the history of sport. Henceforth, for nearly three centuries, governments would look to promoting skill and strength in the use of the new, demanding weapon, while the populace would see it as either competing unfairly with their other leisure pursuits or as a means for creating new archery sports of their own.

The Joust and the Greensward

Medieval lords and commoners led separate but overlapping lives, and this was reflected in their play. The land-owning - and peasant-owning - class had somewhat less discomfort, more warmth, better food, and greater time to play. Nevertheless, many of the hardships of the times were shared. There was the same exposure to illness and early death, the hardness and perils of warfare, and the unremitting demands of the seasons. Time, economic and social advantage, and the need to demonstrate their military preparedness made the sporting activities of the ruling classes different from those of the masses, but the separation was never total. Not only did the peasantry share, albeit in a supporting role, in some of the noble pursuits, but popular sports themselves were often sponsored and supported by the local lord.

The characteristic feature of knightly sports was its concentration on the horse. The capacity to manage the great horse was both a symbol of authority and a practical necessity for travel, for the supervision of the estate, and above all for warfare. Kings, most of all, had to show their might in their great stables. Edward II kept one of his royal studs in the remote Yorkshire castle at Pickering, where he had two stallions, eighteen mares, and a string of younger horses, making fifty in all. The horse was the natural first vehicle for the nobleman's sport, and hunting provided the earliest and commonest of his sporting pleasures.

Hunting may have begun as a necessity for the pot but it soon became a sport for the privileged rather than a means of survival. The remains of medieval deer parks bear witness to the transition. The earliest tend to be small enclosures, usually in distant parts of the estate, and clearly part of its stock breeding. Later parks are larger, surrounding the great house, and equally certainly for amenity value and hunting. The sport took many forms, from the grand chase over the

Hunting the boar, the most prized medieval prey (Joseph Strutt).

ruthlessly cleared and jealously defended royal forests, to polite herding of deer within parks to appointed spots where the ladies might shoot at them, and there could even be temporary grandstands for spectators to watch the kill. Locally, it was usually less staged. The lord of the manor would chase with his spear, his arrows and his dogs, and his villeins would be on hand to flush out the prey and haul it home. Everywhere, though, there were soon some rules. Each prey had its specific season, and its status. The boar was the prime target and remained plentiful through the Middle Ages; the wolf declined rapidly, trapped as well as hunted because of its threat to other animals; foxes were considered very inferior - but all shared the same season, from the Nativity (8 September) to the Purification of Our Lady (2 February).

For horsemen to race against each other must be almost as old as riding itself, but horse-racing remained almost entirely impromptu and informal in the Middle Ages. Records of such events as the race for 'divers knights' over three miles for a £40 purse, in or about 1190 are rare. Steeds bred to carry iron-clad knights into battle were hardly built for speed and although medieval kings had their 'running horses' (and the 'Master of the Running Horses' became effectively the royal racing manager some centuries later) they seem to have been used only for hunting. The majority of medieval horses were much better suited for the knightly sports of the tournament, where competition and military training went hand in hand.

The tourney had become a highly sophisticated sport before the Middle Ages were out. It was a contest between knights who, singly or in teams, charged at each other on their war horses, lances raised, down the long tiltyard. It was a scene which has become a favourite with film directors for its rich panoply of tents, coloured pennants, flashing shields and wimpled ladies. Just as significant, though, were the features often described as 'modern' which were already there in this early sport. There was a precisely delineated playing area, special to the tourney and often enclosed, there were pre-arranged matches; the spectators were well catered for and their role was quite separate from that of the players. There were rules of play, and fouling - such as striking an opponent when his back was turned - was penalised. The scoring was clear-cut, judges decided disputed points, results were often recorded and some are still available today. The tourney, too, was the home of the 'champion,' a very familiar concept today. Although the usual role of the lower orders was to admire from a distance, supplementary entertainment in the tiltyard was sometimes provided by servants fighting each other in semi-serious fashion with blunted poles.

Another sport in which the wealthy took the lead and the peasants acted as their assistants was hawking. This was, moreover, a pursuit which was also open to the medieval lady, who often had her own falcons, just as she had her own greyhounds, a popular present from anyone seeking her favours. Ladies, too, played tennis, in one or more of its several evolving forms. In built-up areas, walls inevitably attracted ball games. One form of hand-ball graduated from the monastic cloister to the castle and the palace, where special courts were built, replicating some of the hazards inherited from the game's original venues. A rude form of 'tenys' was being played in church precincts by the mid-fifteenth century, enough to produce complaints from the cathedral authorities at Exeter and other ecclesiastical sources. This Real (Royal) Tennis soon used the racquet rather than the hand, and is still, of course, played in several courts. For the majority, though, the hand remained the usual implement, and church walls became the chief locations for the game that developed into fives.

For play to release itself from the occasional mass celebration it had not only to find new times but also its own physical space. One of the first sporting areas to establish itself was the bowling green or alley, sometimes in association with the alehouse, sometimes in monastic or castle grounds. Here, early prints depicting the game show the jacks commonly as cones and the bowls were as likely to be thrown as rolled, not surprisingly since the ground was bound to be uneven as the turf could only be kept short by the scythe or the sheep.

How much access the wider public had to some of these bowling places is a matter of guesswork. A space for 'Jousting the Javelin and a Bowling Green,' within Chichester Castle, for instance, was probably fairly exclusive, while the green still in use on the edge of the abbey precincts at Christchurch was likely to have been open, as was that outside the gates of Tewkesbury Abbey. Bowls was certainly one of the sports common, if not always in the same form, to all the classes, and which continued for centuries to defy the class delineation of sports. While there was exclusiveness in some medieval play, it was not until the Tudor period, after the old feudal personal ties between lord and serf had been dissolved, that the concepts of class division and precedence were more formally defined. The overlap between the play of all classes was a natural consequence of upbringing. The young man of the manor was seldom sent away to school but grew up with the servants and shared much of his boyhood playing with them. Popular sport was not the foreign concept that it became to some later ages.

Sponsorship of popular sport became a personal, and in the developing towns, a civic function. From the early thirteenth century there were annual organised wrestling competitions in London, with a ram as the prize, and in the next century there was a regular contest between the officers of the City

The bowling green at Christchurch, within the Priory precincts.

Tewkesbury Abbey

(porters, sergeants, yeomen, and the like) and men from the suburbs, which included Westminster. There were diverse days of wrestling matches at Clerkenwell, and archery at Finsbury Fields. The sport was watched over by the Lord Mayor, Aldermen and Sheriffs, and attracted large crowds - enough in 1222 for a dispute to be inflamed into several days of rioting.

Nor were spectators at sporting events just people from the immediate locality, if the strictures of some medieval churchmen are to be believed. One fourteenth century bishop complained that 'folk go willingly to a long day's occupation, to wrestlings and fairs and spectacles, and vain bodily recreations, while they will scarce trouble to go one mile to hear a sermon.'

It is a view supported by the reports of large crowds attracted to some events away from the capital. A hundred spectators and players were whipped, in lieu of excommunication, after a crowd had supported plays and wrestling in St Albans Abbey churchyard in 1197. At Tewkesbury, opposite the Abbey gateway, a large gathering gave offence when there was skittling and tennis on the new bowling green there in 1469. There were many other such instances in the two and a half centuries between the two episodes. Sporting crowds were common all over the islands. Scotland had at least its full share of communal football games. Apart from the Kirkwall game, there were contests at Jedburgh, Hawick, and Scone, and even one between the married and unmarried women at Fisherrow. Scots also shared with their

English counterparts a popular preference for sports rather than archery practice, to the dismay of their kings. In Ireland, English settlers pursued their old games and traditions - the Ram Fair, or Lammas Fair, at Greencastle, County Down, for instance, had not only its wrestling, boxing, and morris-style dancing, but also echoes of much more distant celebration, with the ram, one of the pre-Christian symbols of midsummer fertility, mounted high on the castle wall.

The attitudes of the ruling class, of the civic and ecclesiastical authorities towards such events, and towards all popular play, were always ambivalent. The perpetual objective of keeping the populace contented enough to accept their lot and fit and ready for any service they were called upon to perform was always likely to be tempered by suspicion of the anarchical nature, the strain of misrule, in much of popular play. For that play to develop it needed a surer basis than the spasmodic sponsorship of the privileged, lay or clerical. From the later fourteenth century onwards that focus was increasingly provided by the alehouse.

Drinking and play have always been closely associated. The great parish feasts at the patronal festival of the local church, as well as the celebrations of Christmas, Michaelmas, and so on, were always occasions for both carousing and play. The church or the manor often sought a monopoly for their own specially brewed ale during these festivals, and there were many local stipulations which ensured both merriment and profit. For instance, at the Deverills, a group of villages in Wiltshire, the thirteenth century practice was for the bachelors to have free ale for as long as they could stand up, but once they sat down they had to pay! Such monopolies, though, along with other feudal restraints were soon to weaken, and the alehouse would come into its own, not only as a place for drinking but as a strengthening thread in the secular fabric of community life. As the church became less central to social life, the alehouse became the focal point for many of the local activities, and particularly for the people's play and recreation. The alehouse began to assume its enduring role as a major provider of sporting opportunities, with its proprietors always more keenly attuned to changes in habits and fashions of play than either governments or, in later days, sports administrators.

The success of the local brewer in catering for the urge to both drink and play was soon apparent in the strictures of those clerics, friars and others, who were emerging on the reformist wing of the church. Langland, the author of *The Vision Concerning Piers the Plowman*, saw the taverns as clear rivals to religion, as haunts of profanity with their gaming tables and their dice. Workmen and craftsmen were drunk at least twice a week, according to another preacher, and always on Sundays - they were tireless in shooting at the butts, drinking, playing at chess and throwing dice, but quite neglectful of spiritual things.

There were clearly changes taking place in the country's social life, and not least in the people's play. It is always dangerous to infer too much from individual events in tracing the history of sport. Human play flows on a deep current which is usually below the surface of any political action and tends to react slowly to economic and social change. The disintegration of the feudal system, though, hastened and confirmed by the labour shortages after the ravages of the Black Death in the mid-fourteenth century, did mark a decisive stage in the expansion and organisation of sport. There was greater freedom of movement, there was somewhat more leisure, and more options as to how to spend it. Local controls were less of a shackle than they had been, and while the manor and the church were still potent forces in people's lives, their authority was less absolute than it had been in the past. It is easy to exaggerate the changes, but they are reflected in the gradual appearance of new forms of play and, indeed, in a new mood in government which, seeing the people's recreational habits as a potential threat to its own long-assumed right to control all aspects of popular behaviour, began its long and still persisting struggle to impose its own constraints on popular sport.

Warrior Kings and Worried Friars
Sport in the later Middle Ages began to achieve its own independent existence. It freed itself from the ties of specific holy days, began to attract spectators, achieved greater variety, and took on more formal shapes. In doing so, it was responding to deep seated changes in the mood of the country. It was not merely a matter of changed material circumstances, a modest rise in living standards - reflected, for example, in the growth of international trade, which spiced up the diet - or even in the loosening of feudal bonds, important as these were for both health and freedom. It was more, too, than the change in political styles which saw, in England in particular, the first hints of the concept of the nation state, with a pride in its communal life. What was happening over much of Western Europe was a change of attitude towards the whole physical world in general and to the nature of the human body in particular, a change which ultimately was to have profound effects on the whole understanding of man's place in the order of things.

The prevailing stance of the Christian church, from the early fathers onwards, had left little room for sport and play. What was tolerated was there for convenience, not from conviction. The church lifted its eyes to the life to come and the material and physical worlds were only seen as ultimately worthwhile if they contributed to the future glory. Chaucer's poor parson might show the positive aspects of this mood, but it was hardly one in which sport and recreation would be encouraged to flourish.

The full reaction against this abnegation of the human body and its potential had to await the Renaissance, yet during the thirteenth century the emphases had begun to shift. Philosophers like St Thomas Aquinas were prepared to grant the body a modicum of worth, while the church itself found compelling needs to acknowledge the value of physical strength in order to protect its own interests. The Teutonic Knights in Northern Europe, and then the crusading orders, which spasmodically sought to wrest Jerusalem from the grip of Islam, developed and maintained a tradition of military training. This military training, in turn, soon produced its competitive versions of combat sports.

As part of Catholic Europe, England could not remain isolated from these changes. The tournament, the central competition of knightly preparation, was given the royal stamp by the crusading Richard I as early as 1194, though its history was uncertain for the next century, even being banned during the minority of Henry III in 1230s. The risk to political stability of having too many fighting men come together in unsettled times was an unnecessary one. As the tournament subsequently became a confirmed part of the sporting life of the ruling class the church itself began to have doubts, and not only about the spiritual value of the tourney and such other knightly sports. There were growing tensions between the high ecclesiastical establishment, pre-occupied with material affairs, and the generations of reforming critics who eventually culminated in Martin Luther. From Langland to Wycliffe, England had its share of these, often with good cause, and both sides of the clerical debate had their implications for the country's recreational behaviour.

The monasteries had played a modest part in promoting popular play. Their bowling greens apart, they were responsible for the introduction of some forms of play, such as, for example, 'Knock-the-devil-down,' which was an early version of bowls. The peasantry were said to have originally stood their clubs up against a wall and then knocked them down with a circular stone. More conspicuous, though, were the sporting activities enjoyed by the monks themselves - and made much of when Henry VIII sought to dissolve the monasteries - from ball games to archery, and the sporting privileges which all senior churchmen shared. King John granted them the right to take a deer on their travels through any of the royal forests, while their zeal for hunting in general was so conspicuous that by the Reformation the See of Norwich alone had accumulated no less than thirteen deer parks among its properties. Since the leaders of the church often came from noble families it is not surprising that they should share the same sporting proclivities as their lay brothers, though the lesser clergy were equally prone to sporting and other pleasures, and all became targets for the critics.

Chaucer's friar in the *Canterbury Tales* was hardly a model of asceticism, but it was from some of his fellows, the wandering preachers, that the fiercest attacks came. Churchmen, peers, and peasants alike came in for castigation, and, incidentally, the sermons of these wandering preachers throw useful side-lights on the sporting habits of the fourteenth century. The nobility were accused of wasting their youth in hunting and jousting 'and all forms of sports and amusements which delight the body,' and, in an age when 'sport' was still only vaguely defined, they were taken to task for their pride 'in having so fair a concubine, for playing well at chess, or for being skilful with the lance or the dice-box.' The common folk were no better. They neglected church and the observance of holy days in favour of the tavern and the call of play. Even the priests were said too often to care more for 'archery competitions, wrestlings and public shows than for the church's sacraments.' Langland warned them to leave hunting to the men at arms, though these knightly gentlemen, in their turn, felt the lash of the preachers' tongues. They had made the tourney a competitive pleasure in its own right, and not the preparation for the Holy Wars that it was meant to be. They were 'carpet-knights' who lurked contentedly at home rather than joining crusades. The tiltyard had been corrupted by expense and indulgence, had lost all spiritual significance and was marred by 'the deaths of men and perils to their souls which often arise therefrom.'

Not for the last time, the sterner minds of the later Middle Ages found the country in terminal moral decline. Luxury, sloth, and indulgence appeared to be in the ascendancy. A little added leisure and a modest rise in living standards could amount to the collapse of all virtue. Women, for instance, became even more evidently the instruments of the devil, with their fashionable slit-sided dresses, 'lascivious and carnal provocation, and the perdition of those who behold them.' Once honourable sports were being corrupted, the tournament losing its old courtesies, becoming sullied with foul language and profanity - tiltyard hooliganism, in fact.

But so far as the broad swathe of sporting behaviour was concerned, this 'sloth' and 'luxury' meant added opportunity. In the records of the fourteenth and fifteenth centuries new games are constantly referred to. Sport became sufficiently important and thus threatening to the authorities, to give rise to growing attempts to keep it in bounds, where time and unremitting labour had applied their own constraints in previous centuries. These attempts to regulate play provide one of the main indicators of the growth and diversification of later medieval sport.

First there were the intermittent efforts of the church, to restrict the playful inclinations of the priesthood, to turn the people's minds from sport to religion, and to preserve some dignity in its premises. The churchyard's popularity as a playing space persisted - its gates serving frequently as 'goals' in communal football, the church walls being used for ball games, and its yew trees, safely enclosed from cattle, were now the source of wood for the archer's long bow. It was to take centuries before play was finally expelled from the churchyard by high iron rails and vigilant Victorian sextons, but attempts began to be made. In the mid-fourteenth century the Archbishop of York banned all commerce and 'wrestlings, shootings or plays.' A hundred years later, instructions to parish priests show that the problem had become more diverse, with a whole range of sports that now called for interdiction - dancing, quoiting, bowling, tennis, handball, football, stoolball, and, in the phrase that was to become a common catch-all, 'all manner of other games.' Priests themselves were told to keep a firm bridle on their sporting activities. The Synod of Ely, for example, in 1364, banned them from hunting, hawking and wrestling, and dicing and gaming led to more than one dismissal from office. Even the mystery plays, for all their religious intention, could seem a dangerous rival to actual worship. Work might keep folk from church, but 'few there are,' according to one censorious friar, 'whose business keeps them from new shows, as in the plays which they call "Miracles".'

These 'shows' were not the only novelty to impinge on the course of popular recreation. Rising property interests began to compete with customary play, especially in built-up areas. The Statutes of King's College, Cambridge might bar the keeping of dogs and falcons, and all gaming, on moral grounds, but they prohibited throwing stones, shooting arrows, or similar behaviour because these might damage the 'window glass' or other parts of the college fabric. The wider use of glass is an early instance of the effect of economic and technological advance in sporting development!

Wider prohibitions sprang from several different interests. In the case of hunting, the statutory controls were a straight protection of privilege, to protect it as a sport against those for whom it might be a vital necessity. The 1390 Game Law excluded all 'artificers and labourers' worth less than 40 shillings a year and 'any priest or clerk' with a preferment of less than £10 a year. It was designed to make hunting very much an elite pursuit, and was backed by attempts to limit the keeping of greyhounds, the main hunting dog, which gave rise to many prosecutions.

Local concerns for law and order lay behind some of the edicts against games playing. Many such local prohibitions reflect government instructions to sheriffs, in the interests of military training, but others were free-standing, a response to particular irritations. At Halifax, for instance, where 'celebrations' were likely to get out of hand even up to the mid-eighteenth century according to a local clergyman, there was a ban in 1450 on dice, bowls and football 'or other unlawful games.' Offenders were to be fined 12d for each offence, and the order was repeated four years later, with an added fine of 4d. There were several successful prosecutions. It was much more expensive to offend at Sherborne in Dorset, where the Manorial Court in 1462 forbade tennis, ball games, cards and kailes under pain of both imprisonment and a fine of 6s 8d. Both places, incidentally, were textile centres, and these may be early hints of the problems that industrialisation was to give rise to centuries later.

While, for the most part, local pronouncements against medieval sport seem to have been made at the behest of government, further exploration of such sources as manorial court records may well correct this view. The preservation of the public peace was certainly a national concern but the crown's new interest in the people's use of leisure and hence their sport sprang from the effectiveness of the long bow as a weapon of war. Training and practice in its use became an overriding consideration - the battles of Bannockburn in 1314 and Crecy in 1346 were highly pertinent events in the history of sport. The English might have lost the first, but it was only after their archers had done great damage at long range, and the success of the long bow was confirmed at the latter. Even before Edward II left for Scotland in 1314 he had prompted the then Lord Mayor of London to forbid 'great footballs in the fields' of the city, but still avowedly in the interest of the 'Preservation of the Peace.'

Thereafter, though, the change of emphasis is clear. Sports are banned not mainly for their public nuisance but because of the interference with archery practice. A series of virtually identical instructions to sheriffs in the 1360s emphasises the point - 'everyone in the shire, on festival days when he has holiday, shall learn and exercise himself in the art of archery' - and the list of games forbidden to ensure that there was time to do this grows longer with every year. It includes throwing games, of stones, quoits, iron bars and the like, handball, football, club- or stick-ball, 'cambus' (which might be a form of hockey), cock-fighting, 'and other vain games of no value.' Some of the local pronouncements of the next century go even further in their descriptions of undesirable games. The Borough Ordinances of Leicester, for instance, as well as forbidding dice, cards, hazards, tennis, bowls and football, add also such pastimes as 'blowing with arrows through a trunk at certain numbers by way of lottery, quoits with horseshoes, pennyprick, (and) . . . checker in the mire, on pain of imprisonment.' ('Penny prick' involved throwing at an upright stick to displace a penny placed on top of it; 'checker in the rye' remains obscure.)

Beyond doubt, play was expanding. The question remains as to the effectiveness of the numerous edicts seeking to confine it. Certainly the Scottish Court thought them worthwhile enough to issue similar edicts in the interests of archery training. During the fifteenth century the first three Jameses all forbade football and other sports, and instructed all males over 12 to practice at the butts. While the lowland Scots never took kindly to the bow and were reported to be 'slack in their obedience,' the highlanders did with gusto and there are later records of their resorting to target practice even at time of divine service. In both kingdoms, the erection and maintenance of the local archery ground became a civic duty, and one that was likely to be enforced, if only intermittently.

Enforcement, though, was never easy. Governments have always found popular play difficult to control, without punitive policing. Medieval kings had few consistently effective policing powers at their disposal and the implementation of unpopular legislation depended very much on local sentiment. There is, in fact, every indication that the edicts against play were emergency short-term measures to meet particular crises rather than sustained and systematic measures of social control. That, at least, was so in effect, if not in intention. The timing of virtually all the orders coincides with some particular military preparation or political unrest. The 1331 edict, for example, came when Edward III assumed the throne after a disturbed regency and was preparing for warlike enterprises in both Scotland and France. The edicts of the 1360s coincide with the high point of his French adventuring, while the 1409 London proclamation came at the time of Owen Glendower's last Welsh foray into the English Marches. Too little attention has so far been given to the specific political circumstances behind sporting legislation, even with the example of the attempts of the 1980s to control football spectators still in mind, and largely motivated by the single will of the Prime Minister. While it could be argued that all the decades of the French Wars and the Wars of the Roses were turbulent, these lengthy confrontations were only spasmodic, and between their phases of fierce conflict there were many years of relative calm. It is reasonable to suggest that during these years popular play went relatively undisturbed, and certainly the continual appearance of new games and sports, and the critical comments on time-wasting, disorder, and irreligion would all support such a view.

Whether he practised diligently with it or not, the long bow standing in the corner of every yeoman's and craftsman's cottage was also the guarantee of a certain liberty. The armies were ceasing to be mere feudal levies, and an armed population was not one to be pushed too strongly by legislation that was, for much of the time, only marginal to national needs. So play had its scope, sport expanded, and the games that the people were evolving became ever more firmly woven into the fabric of their everyday lives.

The Living Past I
There are a surprising number of traces of medieval sport remaining, both in the landscape and in document form, though much has yet to be done to bring these together in a systematic way.

Place names, and particularly field names, sometimes indicate ancient sporting activities. Plaistow and Playford both recall past play, but there are snares - Cricket St Thomas, for instance, derives from 'cruc', meaning a hill, and has nothing to do with the game. Field names are both much more numerous and much more likely to be identified with old sports. Among them are bowlaway, camping close (from one of the early forms of football), dancers' meadow, football butts (an unusual dual venue!), play cross, and playing close. There are opportunities for local research everywhere on this topic. While articles on local field names are often found in the proceedings of local historical and archaeological societies, the sporting significance of field names is often neglected. Equally, 'sport', in the broad sense that we now understand by it, is frequently ignored in indexes compiled by past generations, and so its absence should not discourage any enquiry into earlier sports history. Early estate maps are usually available in county record offices, and the largest scale Ordnance Survey maps may also be helpful.

Street names, too, will often indicate medieval sporting pursuits. One of the most frequent points to the archery ground - there are at least half a dozen referring to Butts in the London area, and twice as many in and around Birmingham. The Bull Stake, where the bull-baiting took place, still appeared on some town maps until the early nineteenth century. In Dorset, for instance, there was a Bull Stake in Dorchester, and a Stake Street in Bridport. These old town plans are the next step, once present-day town maps are exhausted. Then, out in the country, there are numerous medieval deer parks still to be explored, their extent and their distance from the manor house often indicating whether they were primarily for stock breeding or for sport.

A medieval deer park enclosure near Blandford, Dorset. The ditch has been partly filled in over the centuries - the bank, on the right of the picture, would have originally had a paling fence.

Place and field names again provide clues - South Park, Park Wood, Deer Close, and so on. The boundaries are still sometimes clearly identifiable, especially if they have become incorporated into a hedge. They originally consisted of a bank and ditch, the bank having a stake fence, or, later, sometimes a hedge.

Medieval castles and church buildings retain reminders of the sporting activities of their times in many forms. Existing real tennis courts are few, and usually post-medieval, but the one built at Hampton Court Palace in the sixteenth century is both typical and accessible. Castles are worth exploring for signs of cock-pits, animal baiting sites, or ancient bowling greens, as at Lewes, or at Lancaster, which was used by the prison warders in Victorian times. Tiltyards, like that at Kenilworth, will sometimes be identifiable. On a smaller scale, stonemasons and other craftsmen have left evidence of their every day lives, such as in the hunting scene carved over an arch in Lambourne parish church, Berkshire, and the sporting misericord and stained glass illustrations of ball games in Gloucester Cathedral.

As to written records, while original documents present problems of deciphering, many have been translated and published by local history societies, and these are invaluable sources, by no means yet fully exploited by sports historians. Manorial court proceedings, ecclesiastical court cases, borough records, churchwarden's accounts (for references to damage caused by games playing, for instance) can all prove rewarding.

Useful books on medieval sport are, unfortunately, still not easy to recommend, in the absence of any comprehensive history on the period's play. Some of the best material is found in histories of individual sports, such as Percy M. Young, *A History of British Football* (London, 1968) and Alfred H. Haynes, *The Story of Bowls* (London, 1972). There is useful information on Scotland in Robert Scott Fittis, *Sports and Pastimes of Scotland* (Paisley, 1897). For a sense of the broader medieval social scene, H.S. Bennett, *Life on the English Manor: A Study of Peasant Conditions 1150-1400* (Cambridge, 1937) is still hard to better, particularly as it contains William Fitzstephen's account of London sport in 1175, while Peter Clark, *The English Alehouse: A Social History 1200-1830* (London and New York, 1983) is a pleasing account, even if it does somewhat less than justice to the role of the inn in promoting sport in this early period.

2

Reform, Revolt, Purity and Pleasure

During the sixteenth and seventeenth centuries British society, and more particularly English society, achieved a dynamism beyond anything that the Middle Ages had dreamed of. An expanding economy and increasing freedom to explore new ideas in politics and religion meant that whole systems of belief and action were undermined and reshaped. A still mysterious world, moved by unseen forces, became one governed by rational laws. The energy of the times was expressed in its recreation and leisure, with new sports and games, more playing, watching, and gambling, and, alongside these, the most wholesale questioning ever of the moral and spiritual worth of play itself. These were centuries which began in Renaissance pageantry and culminated in the founding of the Royal Society and the Bank of England. The essential conservatism of human play had to be tempered with a new resilience to flourish in a fundamentally changing world.

The Field of the Cloth of Gold
The young Henry VIII met the French king, Francis I, on neutral ground outside Calais in June, 1520, to make peace for all time between the two countries. They were fighting each other again soon afterwards, but it was the grandeur of the occasion that mattered, not its political substance. A few years before Henry had had a similar meeting with the Emperor Maximilian, the titular head of secular Christendom and he now went determined to outdo even the splendour of that occasion. So there was the scarlet and the gold, the rich pageantry, the ostentatious displays of wealth and power. The banners waved and the shields were brave with their bold heraldic devices. The colours, the richness, and the pomp were the essence of the occasion, not its mere trimmings.

Villa Park, for instance, could carry the same echoes when the claret and blue met the gold of Wolves, or Old Trafford when the red and white roses did battle on the cricket field. Indeed, it was a great game as much as the diplomatic event. Heraldic devices still abound on the sports grounds of the land on shirts and flags. The colours and emblems signal an identity, just as they did on the Field of the Cloth of Gold, but there the display was symbolic of a whole gamut of deep-seated changes in English -and subsequently British - social and economic life. In spite of some later excursions

Henry VIII (Pen and ink version by Holbein, from Cassell's *History of England*)

during the rest of the century, it effectively marked the end of attempts to regain the old French possessions. Henceforth, attention would be focused on the British Isles and their relationship to the seas, and the consequent sense of national separateness would begin to thrive and be celebrated. In play no less than in politics there would soon be a national strain firm enough for Shakespeare to know and relish.

The economic fluidity of the Modern Age made for much quicker movement up - and down - the economic and social scale, but at the same time it became important for men to know exactly *where* they were on the ladder. The heraldic blazons outside Calais were thus more than decorations, they were statements of lineage and station. As the power to muster followers ceased to make its own delineation of status, more formal means were called for. The Act of Precedence of 1539, with its precise ranking of court officials, was a symptom of that class awareness noted by the Elizabethan, Thomas Nashe, who claimed that 'the rich disdain the poor. The courtier the citizen. The citizen the countryman. One occupation disdaineth another. The merchant the retailer. The retailer the craftsman,' and so on. It was an awareness that extended to play, at least in the social theorising of contemporary writers, though less effectively so in practice.

Renaissance authors, in their courtly advice, urged a distinctiveness in sport and recreation, imbuing the play of the upper classes with characteristics which would separate it from the unthinking sport of the masses. The ideal gentleman should have the capacities and strengths of the soldier, but he should also be completely at home in the richness of the court, where he would display easy manners, accomplished address, be aware of the classics, able to turn out a passable sonnet - and be skilled in all acceptable games and recreations. While the original inspiration behind this movement was Italian, Britain produced its own courtly writers, like Ascham, with *The Schoolmaster*, Lawrence Humphrey with his *Of Nobilitye*, and above all Sir Thomas Elyot's *The Governour*. They were avowedly aimed at the rearing of the young aristocrat, but they became essays in polite behaviour for the socially ambitious over a wide range. Here were the guides to manners - and prescriptions on appropriate play.

Elyot, whose book was probably the most influential of the new editions that poured from the presses, urged recreative exercise to make 'the spirits of man more strong and valiant' so that all the demands of life came more easily to him. Military training figures prominently in his recommendations for hunting, horse-riding, wrestling and swimming. This last was a novel proposal as swimming was a rare skill and even considered dangerous enough to be banned by the Vice-Chancellor of Cambridge University in the shallow, sluggish waters of the Cam. For Elyot, though, it had military usefulness, as well as the support of classical writers, always a bonus point for Renaissance theorists. He does, none the less, leave room for the purely recreative activity. Tennis is acceptable, played briefly, by younger men. Hawking likewise, though not promoted by the ancients, is seen as taking sportsmen (Elyot does not much concern himself with women) into the open air and at least taking them away from 'other dalliance, or disports dishonest, and to body and soul pernicious.' Dancing, though, is praised for all, as bringing out the essential qualities of both sexes.

Avoidance of 'disports dishonest' was to be one of the distinguishing marks of the gentleman. They included football ('nothing but beastly fury and extreme violence') and both skittles and quoits because they called for little physical exertion and also because they took players into bad company, of little social worth. The ambience of any sport was all-important. The lordling's participation was not merely designed to bring him health and alertness, it was also to underline his superiority over the peasantry, impressing those who saw him managing the hawk or the great charger, a sight which 'importeth a majesty and dread to inferior persons.'

The impact, the impression of leadership and power were vital if the prince was to set the pattern before his people. Henry VIII, in his own eyes the true Renaissance prince, was demonstrating as much in his meeting with Francis, but he was showing it, too, in composing *Greensleeves* and reviving the tourney. In his youth he was an athlete and in old age a spectator, if often a grudging one. He ran races, joined in throwing contests, and wrestled - unsuccessfully, it is said - against his rival monarch. At one of his youthful May Day excursions he made a match against his brother-in-law, the Duke of Suffolk, a race 'on great chargers.' Then, on the way home, in a happy marriage of the old English and the new classical, he was greeted by a Lady of the May, one of whose six attendants was dressed as the goddess Flora.

Italian riding and fencing masters were welcomed (and popularly ridiculed) as an acknowledgement of the origin of the new manners. The marks which Henry and his Tudor successors left on the physical sporting landscape were, however, characteristically British. While the royal bowling alley which he laid down in Whitehall has long since disappeared, his cockpit in St James Park, off Birdcage Walk, was recognisable until the early nineteenth century. Most impressive of all is the tennis court at Hampton Court Palace, where the Tiltyard Gardens are a reminder that the tourney did not have to depend on old medieval sites for its performance.

The tiltyard at Kenilworth Castle. It was here that a lavish entertainment was mounted for Elizabeth I in 1575, including jousting on this long, level space.

Elizabeth I was as eager as her father to set the tone and style of courtly recreation, though the ceremonial often began to overlay the actual contest. The royal hunt became a highly staged ritual designed to allow the Queen to apply the final arrow to an exhausted driven stag. The Queen revised the rules of the tournament and expected to be entertained by jousting on her progresses from one great house to another, though she found that loyalty could sometimes be pushed too far: fewer and fewer of the gentry were prepared to risk their necks in an enterprise which had lost its military value and bouts often became semi-serious affairs between servants wielding blunted poles. Renaissance courtesy remained a powerful influence, but the Tudor gentleman was always prepared to have no more than half an eye for it, and to go his own sporting way. In Scotland, it was golf which brought calumny on the head of Mary Queen of Scots for playing the game too soon after the death of her second husband, Lord Darnley, and south of the border too, upper class sport was often, in practice, pursued at some remove from what the courtly ideal required.

Hunting was by no means always Elyot's gallant chase of the swiftest prey, and deer were prized more for their fatness than the challenge of their speed. If it was excitement hunters were after, they chased the hare. The crossbow was displacing the long bow in the hunt and even the gun was making its appearance on the hunting field later in the century. Henry VIII himself possessed a breech-loading gun but the use of fire-arms for sport spread only slowly - even a hundred years later a marksman who could shoot down a bird in flight was regarded as something of a wonder.

Other changes in weaponry also had their sporting impacts. The old broadsword went out of fashion with the gentry as its military usefulness declined. New fencing weapons and styles were imported from Europe. By the middle of Elizabeth's reign the rapier had become an essential article of attire and fencing lessons had become a staple of the gentleman's education. The duel became such a common means of settling quarrels that the English even won a reputation for hot-headedness. The Queen herself intervened to prevent many proposed duels and sponsored the 1580 law to limit sword lengths to three feet and daggers to twelves inches, still formidable weapons, though, demanding athletic skills in their employment. The traditional sword did survive in one important sporting context, among professional swordsmen. These became a well-organised company, holding contests in inn-yards and on the stage, and attracting large crowds. They usually fought in the 'English' style, with the flat sword and buckler, which made for more obvious excitement and drama (and less chance of serious injury) than the delicate cut and thrust of Italianate styles.

The success of these swordplay bouts in the later decades of the century was symptomatic of the steady commercialisation of sport. Prosperity, the availability of ready money and the readiness to venture with it was not confined to manufacture and trade. It had its mirror in the rapid rise in gambling. Wagering on the outcome of contests was virtually as old as sport itself, but the stakes now grew by leaps and bounds. Henry VIII's largest recorded bowling losses were some £35 in April 1532 (Anne Boleyn lost £12.7s.6d. to the Sergeant of the Cellar the following month). The 2nd Earl of Rutland, at much the same time, was backing his horses to the extent of no more than £1 or £2, while by the 1590s the 5th Earl rarely wagered less than £100 on any of his runners. Every sport attracted more and more gambling money - cock-fighting, archery, bowling, racing of every sort, and swordplay contests. Neither was the betting confined to sports - there was even a book made on whether the Queen would marry or not, with odds of three to one against!

The pristine requirements of the courtly mode of morals and manners were thus only partially preserved. The pull of native sports and recreations was strong, and in some directions it could defy all injunctions aimed at keeping the play of the gentry apart from that of the people. Traditional folk play might have little lordly involvement besides amused spectating and mild patronage, but with the developing sports it was another matter. Two at least of them attracted all classes. Archery and bowls were pursued right across the social range though, admittedly, it is difficult to be certain whether the various classes actually played together. The likelihood is that there was some overlapping of interest, especially as the professional gamester began to appear on the scene. An act of 1541 actually sought to reassert the class distinction in bowling, closing all public greens and alleys and limiting play to gentlemen rated at £100 or more a year, except during the Christmas season. While the prime motive behind the legislation was the usual one of turning athletic energies into archery practice, and was thus doomed at best to short-lived effectiveness, it was at the same time an attempt to reassert the class prerogatives in play, to preserve for the well-to-do their own sporting exclusivity. Where archery was popular it was more often than not in forms which were not of much military value, consisting of shooting at small targets over short distances, which made for much better sport than the long-distance firing, which another of Henry VIII's statutes tried to enforce.

So while richness, splendour, and separateness had their manifestations in the upper-class sport of the sixteenth century, they were far from being its only feature. The Field of the Cloth of Gold heralded only one aspect of the sporting life of the Elizabethan gentleman. There were other currents at work which would have dramatic effects on play and its development. Profound changes were taking place, on the one hand giving more scope for the growth of more sophisticated games and sports, but on the other hand promoting a rising middle and commercial class for whom play tended always to have a lower priority than it did for either their betters or their inferiors. Hand in hand with this new hard-headed seriousness of material purpose, religious change was prompting an examination of whole life-styles, one more thorough-going than any since the early days of Renaissance humanism. The sports of the gentry and those of the people still flourished, often apart, but sometimes together. How long they could continue to do so without question, interruption or change became increasingly a matter for speculation.

Elizabethans at Play

For the time being, though, Elizabeth's subjects enjoyed a growing sporting life and it was to take a new and less revered dynasty before these growing pressures would make their impact on recreation. For many, the second half of the sixteenth century became progressively more dynamic, more thrusting and more profitable. The defeat of the Armada boosted national pride, thriving crafts and adventurous trading brought added wealth, and music and drama flourished. Play could share in the new spirit of enterprise and experiment, without deserting its firm roots in the popular past.

At the parish level - and even large towns remained often no more than a group of parishes, each conscious of its own identity - the sporting year still centred on the local festivals as much as on the national celebrations of Christmas, Easter, and Whitsuntide. The church ale, the patronal feast of the parish church's own saint, and the fair days - these were the recreational landmarks, and their long-standing observance still sustained play activities which were deeply rooted in the past. There was the drinking, the morris dancing, the general merry-making, the folk games, the chasing and the racing. The 'May Games' continued apace, by no means confined to May itself, with the maypole as likely as not to be set up in the churchyard. And so long as a Sunday, outside service time, remained free for play and modest numbers of saints' days were observed (the Sheffield miners enjoyed thirteen, for instance) then there was scope for the people's recreation.

Individual games were still often rooted in this calendar of local play. The Shrovetide football at Corfe Castle in Dorset was associated with the initiation of new freeman marblers who worked the local stone. Other games would be part of wider celebrations, such as those at Guisborough in Yorkshire where the menfolk gathered in the town's Deere Close for annual feasting, 'making matches for horse-races, dog-running, or running on foot,' a typical example of the long transition from a collection of individual sports events towards their emergence as individual contests in their own rights.

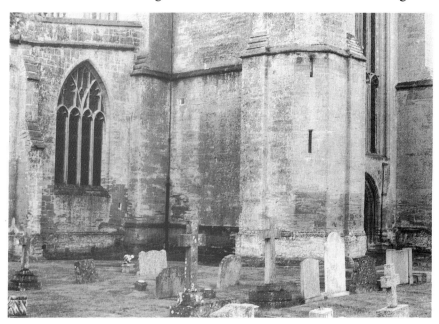

Martock Church, Somerset. Among the churchyard sports was fives, and this was one of many churches which had 'ye fives place' at the base of the north wall of the tower. The steps cut into the buttresses to climb up to retrieve balls from the roof remain identifiable.

The tally holes, used to keep scores.

Popular play was essentially local or regional. In spite of considerable population movement - a frequent hurdle for those seeking to trace their early family history - play forms had no cause to move to any wide uniformity. Only the wealthy and the regular travelling classes could benefit from any nationally defined sport and, indeed, regional variations marked many aspects of life at large. Broadly speaking, the further away from London and the immediate South East, the more loosely was recreation likely to be controlled, though this was to change as local religious attitudes became more diverse. Games playing often developed regionally. In Cornwall the favourite sport was already wrestling, along with a local football variant known as 'hurling' which was a throwing rather than a kicking game. Stoolball, the probable parent of cricket, was popular in Sussex and 'stoball', probably the same game, was being played early in Gloucestershire and other parts of the west country. Geographical features dictated some developing play, most conspicuously skating in the fens. In Scotland, horse-racing appears to have been more regular than it had yet become in England, with annual races at, for example, Haddington, Paisley and Stirling, with a silver bell as the customary prize. The notion that Scots racing was encouraged by the improvement of the local bloodstock through breeding with horses escaped from Armada wrecks has to be speculative, delightful as it would be as an example of the impact of political events on sport! Golf was certainly well established north of the border in the sixteenth century, so much so that the Archbishop of St Andrews was only allowed to maintain a rabbit warren on the links so long as it did not abridge rights to 'play at golf, football, archery, all games and other pastimes as anyone pleases.' Among the Irish sports popular at the same time was hockey, included in a Galway ban in 1527, in the inevitable interests of archery.

Over and above all the national, regional, and local differences, however, London dominated. By 1600 it was estimated already to house some 200,000 souls, making it by far the largest population centre in the islands. The continuing predominance of London, with an urban environment not to be paralleled in other cities before the industrial revolution, encouraged there a precocious growth of sport of all sorts, but particularly of sport as entertainment. The capital would lead the way in the development of sporting entertainment for the next two centuries. Apart from the professional fencing contests, advertised with printed handbills there were crowded gatherings for every sort of acrobatics and juggling, for cock-fighting and animal baiting. The Paris Garden was a regular venue for bear baits, and there were over 1,000 spectators there in 1583 when the grandstand collapsed killing and injuring many of them. Sports came to be seen as possible routes to profit for their promoters, and there is an interesting example in a licence granted by the Queen for a certain Mr Poulter to hold sports around the capital on certain days. The contests to be allowed were archery, foot racing, jumping, and throwing. The licence achieved some notoriety because it sanctioned the games on Sundays, just when pressure was growing against Sunday play, but their interest here lies in the fact that they were expected to be profitable to Mr Poulter, who was said to be poor and with four small children to support. The cash would have come from competitors' entry fees, charges for admission, selling victuals or charging rents for booths - for some or all of these.

The lesson that sport could be profitable could not, of course, be confined to London. The fencers spread themselves to Canterbury and Cambridge, where they were banned, at one time, by the university authorities. Everywhere the alehouse keeper had already made his (or still more often *her*) mark as a provider of popular play and as sports multiplied so did the inn's provision. Cards, dice, and gambling tables figure frequently in court cases involving innkeepers, with more occasional charges of mounting unruly bear- or even ape-baits. Their most usual sporting fare was bowling, in spite of Henry VIII's attempts at prohibition, reinforced equally ineffectively by Mary's 1555 Gaming Act, essentially an anti-sedition law, abolishing alleys and other playing spaces where the disaffected might congregate. In the latter part of the century many inns certainly had their own alleys or greens. The Cheshire innkeeper who kept bowls in his house 'and doth suffer the same to be used and bowled with on a piece of ground called the Skyre Heath' had many a fellow, notwithstanding the dire warning that 'by means of which men servants and children are provoked to unthriftiness by the evil example of all others.'

Bowling was a generic term increasingly used to identify a whole family of games which eventually settled into two main forms - skittles, as an alley game, and the green bowls known today. Kayles was clearly the ancestor of the former, with kayle pins becoming kettle or kittle pins, and then skittles. In closh, the bowl was used as a missile, thrown rather than rolled, something like the French boule. With loggats, yet another early form, bones were originally used for both the targets and the missile, before they gave way to more regular bowls. Billiards, too, probably shared the same family ancestry as it seems once to have been a game played on grass, and Charmian's reference in *Antony and Cleopatra* shows that it was well known to Shakespearian audiences.

The bowling alley had advantages over the green for the alehouse keeper. The long planked alley could readily become just a bare room if interference threatened, and even that was less likely if the noise and the crowd could be contained within doors. As the law relaxed, more greens were created in towns, to add to those which had long existed in the greater houses. They appeared, for instance, at Chesterfield, Hadley (Worcestershire), Newbury, Torrington, and at Old Basing, Hampshire, where the great castle of the old town was razed to the ground by Cromwell. The popularity of the games, the familiarity of all classes with its terms, is evidence by the appearance of words like 'bowl,' 'bias,' and 'jack' on the lips of lords and commoners alike, and to judge from the Shakespearian allusions it has to be regarded as the national game of the time south of the Tweed.

On the other hand, Shakespeare echoed the generally received polite view that football was an uncouth game, a sign of social inadequacy. Calling Oswald in *King Lear* 'a base football player' was an apposite insult for an upstart steward. In spite, though, of this widespread denigration, there are signs, outside the mass communal contests, of both some measure of organisation in the game and of gentry involvement. The Cornish hurling game, for instance, was said to be usually set up by local leaders, and there were obviously some standing fixtures - a knightly character in one of Chapman's plays wished to get married so that he could participate in the 'forthcoming great match of football' between the married men and the bachelors. There were known noble footballers, players and fans: Lord Willoughby of Eresby and the Earl of Sunderland joined their servants in a match against an *equal* number of countrymen; the young Viscount Dorchester was invited to a friend's house with the promise of football as one of the main entertainments, while in Scotland the future 7th Earl of Argyle had quite a reputation as a player.

It was clearly not always a contest between vast mauling masses. Restrictions on football at the University of Cambridge in the early 1580s, after a violent affray at a neighbouring village, still allowed it to be played within the precincts of the colleges and confined to members of that college. Given the limited grounds and relatively low numbers at most colleges, a small-scale game must have been feasible. This was the solution suggested by the most practical of the home-grown Renaissance education theorists, Richard Mulcaster, who recommended that the game should be more closely regulated, with a referee to sort the players 'into sides and standings,' to forbid rough play and the 'shouldering or shoving one another so barbarously.' From such comments, it seems more than likely that Mulcaster was aware of the well-organised form of the game being played in Italy by young Florentines. Here, *calcio* - still the Italian name for football - was at its most flourishing around 1600, as a game for upper-class youths, a colourful and ordered contest which even had its specialised players and set formation. The teams had 27 men with 15 forwards (*innanzi o corridori* - 'front runners!') and a 3 - 4 - 5 defence.

So far as Britain was concerned such regulated contests were doubtless the exception rather than the rule. The indigenous style of mass competition was both widespread and not without its value as an escape valve for the settling of old scores - village rivalries or town and gown jealousies. Like much other inherited play, it provided one of those occasions for the suspension of normal restraints on which the health of a restrictive society depends. The annual countryside contests were left to go their own way, largely undisturbed. In the towns, change was making such play less acceptable, with its potential and actual damage to property. Manchester was one of several towns to become concerned about broken windows and imposed a 12d fine on players, though the game was hard to put down completely. Foreign visitors were regularly surprised to come across football in town settings, one Parisian finding it 'not very conveniently civil in the streets,' and generally making comments which pointed to the game as a common pursuit rather than a single annual festive contest.

Other games of the time have similar characteristics, a varying mix of Renaissance tone, plebeian elements, and a tendency to take on several forms. Tennis, for instance, was at its high point of courtly acceptability, an exclusive diversion with its own specialised court. Yet it was also a game played in less sophisticated fashion. Another French visitor in 1588 was surprised to find working men playing for money, and on a working day, while the battledore was common enough for bats to appear as evidence in a Lancashire assault case!

All in all, the Elizabethans enjoyed a flourishing sporting life. They took both the inherited folk games and, to an extent, the new spirit of Renaissance sport and adapted both into play forms which suited their own social conditions and their own apportionment of leisure, large or small. Yet there were already signs that sport and play would come under closer scrutiny. Religious, economic and social changes were all combining to question the nature of recreation and also the occasions when it should be pursued.

Sport and Religion

When Henry VIII broke with Rome and assumed the headship of the English Church he had no intention of fundamentally changing his subjects' religious habits and still less of interfering with the ways in which they enjoyed themselves. It was not until the introduction of the English Prayer Book and, above all, the English Bible that this was to have dramatic consequences, eventually fuelling new attitudes towards belief and behaviour in much the same way as the monastic properties fuelled the land market and encouraged greater social mobility. The English reformation, at government level, remained thoroughly conservative, but it was a conservatism that was generally tolerant and this tolerance allowed a new and potent force to emerge - that of Puritanism.

Those who wished to push further along the Protestant road were excluded from high office and influence, but were left free to speculate. Unlike their fellow reformers on the Continent they did not have religious and political responsibility thrust upon them. They did not have to become administrators overnight whose last concerns, public order apart, would be over play and recreation. It was in England, where there were no distractions by way of everyday political decision-making, that Protestantism led the way to a new interpretation of the place of sport and play. Yet it was not an interpretation which held much encouragement for either.

The study of the Bible might leave no room for popes and little for bishops, but it left equally little room for amusement and play. There were to be no easy pathways to heaven through formal absolutions or bought indulgences. The gates to salvation could only be opened by what a person believed, thought, felt and *did* during his earthly life. Life was so short that every minute of it should, ideally, be spent in active preparation for the hereafter. There were many ways in which worthiness for eventual salvation would show - not only in prayer and worship, but in a godly domestic life, in family training, in help to others, in good example, and in hard, honest work. Play did not figure in the recipe.

Much of Elizabethan play did not, admittedly, ring with the tunes of virtue. It appeared all the worse to those not disposed to give much credence to earthly joys, to the pleasures of exertion and contest, or the enriching possibilities of communal participation. They saw its unruly excitement, the swearing and the gambling, the drinking and the dancing, and the licence that went with the close concourse of men and women together. The phallic significance of the maypole made it a conspicuous abomination, an open target for attack in all that it stood for. By the 1570s Puritan disgust with the recreational activities they saw around them spilled over into printed sermons, tracts, and broadsheets. Philip Stubbes' well-known *Anatomie of Abuses* has a whole catalogue of condemnations, from 'this murthering play' of football to 'this stinking idol' of the maypole; John Dod saw hounds and hawks, cards and dice as a sign that there was 'some sick soul in the family;' and William Hinde found even a foot race 'an exercise of profaneness' with its crowds, its betting, brawling, and quarrelling.

The old folk festivities of Maying were particularly castigated for their pagan associations and for the opportunities for immorality they brought with them. One preacher accused the merrymakers of dancing 'with disordered gestures, and with monstrous thumping of feet, to pleasant sounds, to wanton songs, to dishonest verses. Maidens and matrons are groped and handled with unchaste hands, and kissed and dishonestly embraced: the things, which nature hath hidden, and modesty covered, are oftentimes by means of lasciviousness made naked, and ribaldry under the colour of pastime is dissembled.' The consequences, he went on, were that 'many maidens have been unmaidened,' and, in sum, these festivities were 'the storehouse and nursery of bastardy.' While the Puritans asserted the overwhelming pre-eminence of God as the ruling force in earthly life, they could not emphasise enough the influence of the devil, who readily found work for idle hands, let alone for other parts of the human anatomy.

Even without these purple stains of sin, though, play would have had a hard time of it. The Puritan ethos denied the worth of any activity which was solely satisfying for the pleasure it brought, which of itself effectively squeezed out the play element. Not that they despised the body as such. For them, there was no resigned medieval abnegation of the material and physical worlds for the body had to be kept fit enough to do God's work on earth and to do it with a positive vigour. Daily labour, though, and the pursuit of helpful good works would, for most, keep the body healthy without resort to unseemly recreations. While their attitude was, at root, neutral towards man's physical being, it became anti-sport because of the nature of much contemporary play, and also as a growing antipathy developed towards its traditional occasions.

The holy days had been, and were still, the customary days for play. Sunday, after worship, and the Saints' days scattered liberally about the calendar were the accepted opportunities for sports and games. Now both would come under pressure - Sundays as a day too sacred to be polluted with play, and the Saints' days as blasphemous relics of Catholicism. The Puritans did not discover Sunday but they did elevate the Lord's Day to a sanctity unknown to previous Christian ages. The preaching friars, while they castigated those who allowed unsuitable sports to draw them away from Sunday worship, found no objection to play as such after service time. Sports and games continued to be regarded, until well after the Reformation, as suitable Sunday recreations so long as they did not encroach upon the church's services. This was the common early Protestant stance, with Martin Luther himself insisting that all days were equal occasions for holiness, and rejecting any notion of Sunday as a rest day for any cause beyond mere convenience.

The diligent searching out of biblical texts led the English Puritans to quite other views. The fourth commandment, to 'Remember the Sabbath Day, to keep it holy,' might appear to be sufficient injunction, but Puritan theology eventually went far beyond this. In its most extreme form it argued that the holiness of Sunday did not just depend upon the commandments but stemmed from the Creation itself, when the Lord rested on the seventh day. It was thus the very first of all commands to be observed by true Christians. Nor did the reasoning stop there. Scrutiny of the Bible, while it sanctified the Sabbath, produced no justification for the observance of Saint's days and the other customary church festivals. This came as no surprise to the stern-minded, for how could a serious and diligent life be maintained with so many approved occasions for idleness?

Given the prevailing mood of the times, and particularly the strong anti-Catholic sentiment of the 1580s when the country was under threat from Spain, Saints' days could readily be seen as the inventions of the Pope, prompted by his ally, the Devil. They had been deliberately set up to seduce folk into sin, and both their association with the medieval past and the licence they afforded for offensive merrymaking confirmed their falsity. The fact that Catholic Europe was putting some of its Counter-Reformation energies into the conscious promotion of pageantry, sport and celebration on both feast days and Sundays made the opposite seem all the more morally and spiritually correct to the Puritans. Moreover, a new look at the pattern of work and leisure had a very practical appeal. The gradual industrialisation of English towns made a working week shorn of incidental holidays and with one regular rest day seem extremely attractive, particularly to craftsmen and manufacturers, a group in which Puritans were most strongly represented.

The consequences of Puritan attitudes towards play and the leisure calendar were wholesale in theory and dramatic in practice. Had they prevailed completely not only would virtually all the customary recreations have disappeared but along with them, all the traditional occasions for their enjoyment. Sunday would be free of work, but it would also be closed for play, and the feast days would be no more. Only at some times and in some places was there thorough-going application of Puritan theory, but the long-term impact of this scrutiny of the nature of sport was to persist for centuries to come, and still has its echoes today.

On a local level, a reforming clergyman backed by sympathetic magistrates could make quite drastic changes to popular recreation, and there are many examples of such action from up and down the country. What might appear as an unattractive creed none the less held a strong appeal for those who saw themselves as people of a new age - enterprising, progressive, and individualistic - and for whom the old corporate traditions of the past had come to seem little more than heretical anachronisms. At a time when preaching within the Anglican church was at a low ebb, the Puritan ministers brought a vivid and colourful message, and attempts by Archbishop Laud and his high church followers at revival only served to exacerbate the conflict. Issues such as the

Richard Baxter still looks over Kidderminster, where he eventually succeeded in bringing his parish to godliness. As one of its later defenders, his writings on Puritanism had great long-term influence.

siting of the communion table in the church became entangled with questions over church ales and Sunday sport. In Lancashire, where the new movement came into particularly sharp conflict with a strong residual Catholicism, there were numerous prosecutions for Sabbath-breaking, though many of them can only be identified as such by reference to the calendar. The Middlesex Quarter Sessions records tell the same story. In Lancashire it was music and dancing that gave most frequent offence. In Middlesex much of the contention centred around bowling. In both regions dicing, card-playing, drinking, and the general rowdiness of taverns were tackled with some vigour.

Puritanism was predominantly an urban phenomenon which never struck deep roots in the areas of traditional agriculture but its effects tended to be felt wherever enterprise marked the local economy. One cameo from the Worcestershire records illustrates the problems that competing cultures could bring in the turbulent years of the early seventeenth century. The magistrates there were generally immune to the new restrictive attitudes towards Sunday play - the county had, after all, had strong connections with the Gunpowder Plot. Neighbouring Gloucestershire, on the other hand, was, by the standards of the day, relatively industrialised, and its justices took a stricter view of the Sabbath proprieties. The thwarted inhabitants of two north Gloucestershire villages got into the habit of moving across the county border to Longdon, in Worcestershire, and bringing their Sunday revelries with them, creating noise and near riot, defying the local constables with violence if attempts were made to quieten them. The episode is instructive, not only in revealing the difficulty of policing unpopular edicts. The invaders, for all their irreverence, would cease their play while the service was taking place in Longdon church - though they once pushed an excommunicated woman through the doors, knowing that the worship could not continue with her present, and so the merry-making could resume!

Where Puritan local authorities applied their policies thoroughly, it seems there was acceptance, or at least apathy, among much of the population. To secure national implementation of the new social policies, however, was another matter, especially as the policies themselves became more extreme and demanding.

Fordington Church, Gloucestershire. It was from here that the villagers absconded into Worcestershire for a more cheerful Sunday.

Even during the Commonwealth, after the defeat of the Royalists and the execution of the king, it did not prove easy to apply all the recreational constraints which strict godliness required. The repetition of edicts against play came with a regularity reminiscent of the old prescriptions for archery practice, but now they came virtually every year. There was still an element of national security in the motives behind them, in preventing the gathering of possibly seditious crowds - though they were primarily seen as the means of bringing the country to a proper sobriety. First, there was the parliamentary ordinance of 1644, bringing a total ban on a wide range of sports at any time on the Sabbath, and requiring the destruction of all maypoles. The next year's ban extended the list of forbidden sports to include football and stoolball. Cricket, incidentally never appeared in the catalogues of outlawed activities and this, it has been argued, aided its growth during the Commonwealth years. More probably, the game was too localised or too infrequent to demand specific mention. There were certainly, however, indictments for Sunday cricket playing and Cromwell certainly ordered the destruction of all cricket bats in Ireland, though perhaps because they looked too much like shillelaghs!

Even comprehensive prohibitions of sports and games were not enough for the purists. In 1650 the Commons sought to ban such Sabbath desecration as 'idly sitting, openly, at gates or doors or elsewhere,' or even 'walking in churchyards,' and the clause was only lost by one vote and this because it was thought impracticable, not undesirable. In fact they did bring in a ban some years later on 'vainly or profanely walking' or even the ringing of bells for pleasure on the sabbath. All such restrictions were directed in the first instance at Sunday behaviour but, given the abolition of other holy days and the general tone of Puritan pronouncements, they effectively meant the cessation of most recreational activity. This was not lost on the law-makers themselves, who showed an occasional awareness of the need to provide some outlet for the energies of the young at least. They were cautiously granted a monthly mid-week holiday, though one hedged with conditions about tippling and being out late at night, and, even so, at the discretion of employers.

How effectively all the bans were applied in parishes up and down the land is difficult to judge. Thorough-going opposition to republican government was only stirred up when Cromwell sought to impose central policies with a firmer hand through the appointment of his regional major-generals in 1656. His reasons then were more closely related to security than to piety, and he personally seems to have been more tolerant of sport than many of his party. A keen horseman and hunting man, his own opposition to race meetings, cock-fights and bear baits was largely pragmatic, since at least one royalist plot had been hatched at a pretended hunting party. Yet the antagonism aroused by the new efficiency in local administration under the army officers was more related to the means than to the policies themselves - the cost and pressures of a standing army, the forced billeting, and the high taxation. While many Puritan restrictions were doubtless irksome, the quieter Sunday certainly had its appeal, and restraints on play were only truly oppressive when tight control meant that there was no chance of occasional evasion. There are many instances of continued play during the Commonwealth years, particularly among the upper classes (Evelyn's diary alone has several examples) and Sessions records even report occasional celebrations of the old feast days.

There was little doubt that the restoration of the monarchy would be accompanied by the throwing-off of the formal constraints which the years of godly government had imposed, but history was to show, and to show with surprising rapidity, that much of the Puritan message had entered the national soul, and particularly so where play behaviour was concerned. A new sense of seriousness meant that if ever sport was to achieve widespread acceptance across all sections of society it had to shed its associations with rowdiness, gambling, bad language, dishonesty, and general immorality. Puritanism brought a new strain of asceticism, always at odds with the appeal of play, which left behind a feeling that, ultimately, sport ought not to be too exclusively enjoyable, that it ought to mean taking knocks and bruises as part of the price of its pleasures. The hacking of the shins on the Victorian football field and the virtually unprotected batting against an unforgiving hard ball on the cricket pitch were part of the inheritance.

More immediately, Puritanism brought a reaction against cruel animal sports. In spite of Macauley's complaint that the Puritans objected to bear-baiting not because it gave pain to the bear but because it gave pleasure to the spectators, the truth is that a number of Puritan writers did make a defence of animal rights. The closing of the London bear-pits, never to be re-opened, was only the first step in a long and still incomplete struggle to prevent the exploitation of animals for sport. It was to take two centuries before legislation began to ban animal sports, and some, like fox-hunting, still enjoyed a spurious and precarious legality after the narrow defeat of the Wild Mammals Bill in February 1992. Henceforth voices would always be heard against such exploitation and animal-fighting and baiting would be gradually eroded and hedged in, more and more driven to the rougher and more raffish areas of the country's sporting life.

The other major contribution of Puritanism to sport was to make it, for the first time, a subject of serious national debate. The motives and the approach to the topic might, on the one side, be almost wholly critical and negative, but they meant that play was given consideration as to its nature and its value, and such criticism prompted defence. Given the political tensions of the times, with its inevitable interaction between religion and politics, the debate over sport became political as well as religious. This political debate was as important as the religious one. There is still futile pleading to 'keep politics out of sport,' but since sport is part of the art of living together - the essence of politics - they are bound to be integrally linked. Sport has been a political issue in these islands since at least Elizabethan times and its important role in the great constitutional conflict of the seventeenth century is indisputable.

Stuart Kings: Sport as Politics

For the first thirty years of the Stuart period, sport was closer to the centre of the English political stage than it has ever been since. Against the debates of those years the concern of the 1980s for the control of football crowds seems no more than marginal. Sport in the early seventeenth century became a significant focus for the growing conflict between the crown and parliament that culminated in the English Civil War, the execution of Charles I and the establishment of a republic. Though the real struggle was not over sport itself - even the surface issue was not so much sport as Sunday observance - the implications for the role of play in English society were far-reaching, with considerable and distant consequences. The root political controversy was over whether authority in the state lay with the crown or with parliament, and sport provided a convenient and relatively safe channel through which to pursue the struggle in its early stages. It provided a format for sustained shadow-boxing, until the gloves came off in the 1630s, when the real conflict came out into the open. Then sport was relegated to the sidelines until the war was won and lost.

There had been signs in the last years of Elizabeth I's reign of a growing restiveness among many members of the House of Commons. Equally there were signs that Sunday behaviour, and particularly Sunday play, would be one of the topics on which they would seek to assert their independence of the crown. The Commons, more inclined to a radical version of Protestantism than the crown, and increasingly commercial in its interests, was concerned over its lack of any real control over money supply and spending. The members had no wish to seem innovative, let alone revolutionary. Both they and the crown were claiming only what they held to be their traditional rights, and in the control of sport there was ready-made room for dispute. Parliaments had frequently legislated on it in the past, albeit usually at the behest of the crown in favour of archery practice, while the crown could equally claim the precedent of numerous royal proclamations on the same theme. Thus there were some tentative parliamentary attempts around the turn of the seventeenth century to exercise greater restraint over Sunday habits. These all foundered on the Queen's opposition to parliamentary interference. Elizabeth was too well respected - and too old - to be seriously challenged over such issues.

This was not the case, however with her successor, a newcomer from north of the border. James I was of another stamp, too, from the old Queen. The Tudors may well have believed in their God-given right to rule the country as they thought fit, but they were careful never to make too much of it in theory, however thoroughly they achieved it in practice. With a King who was always ready to pronounce his divine right to Kingship, opposition from parliament was inevitable. His first parliament at once set about trying, as its very first business, to control the Sabbath, and it became an invariable habit with its successors. Bills to limit Sunday play were passed by the Commons with unfailing regularity whenever they were allowed to meet - in 1606, 1614, 1621, and 1624. They either failed to get through the House of Lords or, if they did, James refused to sign them.

Such a concentration on Sunday sport calls for explanation. Surely there were matters of more immediate moment to which the members might have turned their minds? The answer has several strands to it. A sober Sunday was making its appeal not just to religious interests but also to employers attracted by a more regular working week, to administrators who saw it as a means of improving law and order, and to those who saw it as a legitimate channel through which to voice their constitutional opposition to absolutism. The Sunday Observance bills were the one catalyst which could bring all these forces together. As for the Puritans themselves, they were never more than a minority in the Commons and here was an issue near to their hearts and capable of winning wider support.

Their chance came when Charles I came to the throne, and was desperately in need of funds. He had, as the price of taxation, to accept the inevitable bill, and so the 1625 Sunday Observance Act found its way on to the Statute Book - where it remained until 1969! Determination to secure such an Act had been hardened by James I's actions towards the end of his reign, and particularly by his *Declaration of Sports*. This was issued as a proclamation at Greenwich on 24 May 1618, and was the royal response to complaints he had received, while visiting Lancashire, that local justices were restricting Sunday activities beyond what the law required.

The *Declaration*, or the *Book of Sports* as it became known, did in fact amount to little more than a statement of the existing legal position. Restrictions, he claimed, were hindering the conversion of Catholics, driving the common people to drunkenness, idleness and discontent, as well as denying them the exercise needed to keep themselves 'fit and able' for war. James also made the valid but seldom-mentioned point that if folk could not play on the holy days, they had little opportunity to play at all. Those who did not go to church were 'unworthy of any lawful recreation,' but for churchgoers there was to be a reasonable ration of approval Sunday enjoyment, 'such as dancing, either men or women, archery for men, leaping, vaulting, or any other such harmless recreation.' May-games, church ales, morris dancing and maypoles were all sanctioned, so long as they did not impede Divine Service.

In its content the proclamation was far from radical. For James, it was not only an assertion of his constitutional right to make such pronouncements, but also a personal statement of his own view of himself as a Renaissance sportsman, the man who had introduced the new games of golf and pall mall to England, the keen huntsman who had established a hunting lodge at Newmarket, which was to become the home of British horse-racing. He did not see himself as granting any new freedoms. Bear-baiting and bull-baiting, as well as stage plays, were still specifically prohibited, and so, 'for the meaner sort of people by law prohibited' was bowling. Indeed the *Declaration*, added a new restriction, designed to appeal to the upholders of law and order, to the effect that games were to be confined to the home parish and not to be an excuse for large gatherings, and no offensive weapons were to be carried. The Worcestershire villagers could feel that their complaints were vindicated!

The nature of the dispute over Sunday play is underlined by the similarity between the Sunday Observance Act that parliament passed in 1625 and the King's declaration of seven years earlier. The differences between the two are minimal. The Act merely added legal force to movement out of the parish for Sunday play and laid down penalties for infringements. It was not the content of what James had said that gave offence, but the fact that the king had said it, and the circumstances of brooding antagonism in which he did so. It was an important incident in the constitutional and religious struggle and was to play a spasmodic, and sometimes bizarre role in the future history of sport. The *Book of Sports* was frequently reprinted as a counter to later attempts to constrain Sunday play and was actually quoted in evidence to the Parliamentary Committee on the topic in 1831, as still having relevance.

The practical effects of both the *Declaration* and the Act in the years leading up to the Civil War are difficult to assess. The struggle became predominantly a local one. Parliament made a further assault on Sunday behaviour through the

A Victorian view of the conflict over Sunday play (from Cassell's *History of England*)

1627 Act, concerned solely with trade, but further debate on this favourite topic was cut short by the 'great business' of the Petition of Right. The Commons' constitutional claims were now put squarely before the crown, and sport had to retire to the sidelines.

While the local influence of Puritan employers and magistrates doubtless continued to strengthen during these years, there was powerful pressure from the centre as Archbishop Laud sought to pull the Church of England back towards its Catholic origins. One notable episode in the confrontation concerned the annual parish wakes in the west country. In 1632 the magistrates of Somerset - another county with an element of early industrialisation in its wool and leather trades - petitioned the Lord Chief Justice over the disorders caused by the frequent parish festivals in the county, and they issued their own ban. These wakes, celebrating the patronal saint of the local church, were part religious in that they brought the largest congregation of the year and the largest collection, usually in aid of a specific project, such as repairing the bells or the fabric. They were also occasions for drink, revelry, and unruliness, as well as boisterous sports and games. In the eyes of many, they came too often. But to Archbishop Laud they were an essential part of the old church traditions which he was bound to uphold, in spite of his own personal lack of any sporting instincts - he regarded being bounced about in his carriage as all the physical exercise he needed. So he enquired of the Bishop of Bath and Wells whether his parish priests had reported any disorders to him. Dutifully, the Bishop replied that they had not. Laud confronted the Lord Chief Justice with his findings and had the order revoked.

Matters did not end there. Charles felt that a stiffening of court policy was needed to check these local prohibitions, and so he made the divide between the two sides even deeper by re-issuing his father's *Declaration*, this time adding specific approval for parish feasts. This time, too, the *Declaration* was to be read in all churches. In practice, it was not and many priests lost their livings for failing to do so.

There is growing evidence that some of the old festivals and the play associated with them did revive spasmodically in the 1630s, only, of course, to be snuffed out again with parliament's victory in the Civil War. This is unsurprising. The traditionalist cause was far from being without its friends and was almost certainly more to the taste of the usually silent majority - silent, that is, when they were not making merry. Shakespeare had numerous anti-Puritan jibes, and there was a considerable flow of anti-Puritan writing from the presses. There were, too, the occasional practical steps taken to keep the old recreational practices alive, and even to restore what was thought to have been lost. The court never lost its habit of seeing Sunday as a day for banquets, entertainments, masques, and dancing. Much business was still transacted on the Sabbath, and fairs and markets flourished, in spite of repeated attempts to close them down.

The most conspicuous conscious revival was devised by Robert Dover who, around 1612, began his 'Cotswold Games' on what is now Dover's Hill, above Chipping Camden. Whitsuntide games had been held there for generations in the past but had withered under Puritan attacks, (it was from this part of Gloucestershire that the frustrated villagers were to invade the Worcestershire Sunday a few years later). Dover made a deliberate attempt to set up a celebration which would involve all classes, the gentry as well as the peasantry. He was one of the earliest to appreciate that what was on the surface a religious conflict over play was also a class issue. To attract his social equals, he included hunting, gaming, and chess (though this was played in alehouses almost as much as in gentry parlours). The popular events combined a traditional rusticity - leaping, leap-frog, and shin-kicking - with more forward-looking contests such as pitching the bar and throwing the hammer, together with the usual wrestling, and foot races for men and women. The success of the games was such that it prompted the first anthology of sporting verse in the English language, *Annalia Dubrensis*, which brought together such major poets as Ben Jonson and Michael Drayton, as well as other lesser luminaries. All lauded Dover's flourishing enterprise, praising particularly its harmony and good order, so important at a time when, in the words of one of them,

'All public merriments, I know not how,
Are questioned for their lawfulness.'

By the time that Charles I reissued his father's *Declaration of Sports* much more than public merriments were being questioned as to their lawfulness. It was the whole nature of the country's government. The opponents of sport would eventually have their day under the Commonwealth, and there would be that first exercise in the wholesale control of sport and recreation - before a second Charles came into his own again.

The Living Past II

Tudor and Stuart sport has not left many immediately apparent traces on the physical landscape, though as archaeology continues to strengthen and broaden its interest in medieval and later periods it is likely that more will be revealed. Town digs, for instance, could well uncover a bowling alley, but much sport of the period required little by way of permanent specialised structures. Some earlier features did continue to be important, certainly in the sixteenth century when cathedrals were still being built, tiltyards renovated, and new tennis courts appearing in a few great houses, such as that at Falklands Palace, in Fife, dating from 1539. There are bowling greens, too, attached to some country houses which lay claims to Elizabethan associations, though these tend to rely rather more on surmise than evidence.

Some of the survivals from the Stuart period are on more solid ground. The Mall, in London, remains as a reminder of the game of pall mall, roughly a cross between croquet and hockey, introduced to England by James I and his court. The broad, straight pathway of The Mall gives an impression of the amount of space needed for the game, for which no other sites have been identified in Britain. John Evelyn did record several on the Continent during his exile in the 1650s, comparing one unfavourably for having a curve in it. Newmarket may have little remaining of its earliest years, but it does have its racing museum, and many existing courses on traditional recreational sites (such as Worcester and Warwick) were doubtless in use for racing by the end of the period.

The site of John Dover's games is now well marked by the National Trust. Dover's Hill, as it became known, adjoins the Western-sub-Edge to Chipping Camden road, still has its revived Cotswold Games during Whitsuntide week, with a representation of Dover's original 'castle' erected as a backdrop. Many of the other 'revivals' which became a feature of the 1980s have less validity.

Dover's Hill,
Gloucestershire

Pancake Day races, for instance, are usually recent innovations ('traditions' have always been capable of growing within a few years) and have to be justified by the fun they bring and their profit to charities, not their relevance to sporting history. The cult of 'heritage', however, does raise the wider issue of whether a theme-park Britain is being constructed, with often only tenuous links with the real past. After all, for one thing, most of the Tudor and Stuart past must have stank to high heaven. Apart from the Yorvik Centre at York, heritage rarely smells.

While there is a comparative dearth of artefacts from this period, this is compensated for by an increasing richness in the written evidence, including such contemporary texts as Sir Thomas Elyot, *The Governour* (1531), Roger Ascham, *Toxophilus* (1545), on archery, and Henry Peacham, *The Compleat Gentleman* (1622). As against the considerable literature that touches on elite sport, there is growing insight on popular play to be found in legal and administrative records. From the 1530s local justices were required to come together quarterly on a county basis, and the records of these sittings are quite often available in published form from the later years of the century. These, and the continuing medieval records, give insights into how sporting habits could differ from place to place, and how both they and the attitudes of the authorities changed from time to time. Archdeacons' courts became involved in the religious disputes over play, and their records, where available, must have valuable evidence still untapped.

A reminder of the great age of emblazons and quarterings is still there in the heraldic devices used in the badges of many sports clubs and associations. They may tend to be displaced by modern logos, but many remain, and their heraldic and sporting significances are both well worth exploring. Less tangibly, the social and moral values of Puritanism have been a persistent, if fading influence, both of themselves and through what they have produced. The Sunday sport issue is now settled to all intents and purposes. The final obstacle disappeared with the legalising of the Sunday opening of betting shops in 1995, so making fully functioning Sunday horse racing possible. However, some impacts of the long dispute over the sporting calendar may still be found locally, in spite of the levelling out of holiday patterns in the last half century. The parish church's Saint's day may still be marked by some traditional celebration, possibly a local fair, or older people might remember some such events from their childhoods.

In sport history, Dennis Brailsford, *Sport and Society: Elizabeth to Anne* (London and Toronto, 1969) was the first text to cover the period as a whole but others now include particularly Derek Birley, *Sport and the making of Britain* (Manchester and New York, 1993). Among individual sports that appeared for the first time, horse-racing is well served by Richard Onslow, *Headquarters: A History of Newmarket and its Racing* (Cambridge, 1983), a beautifully produced volume, particularly informative of those early days, when the sport was dominated by Newmarket. In spite of the fact that, of all British sports, cricket is the best documented, there is no entirely satisfactory social history of its earliest years, and probably the most useful remains Roland Bowen, *Cricket: A History of its Growth and Development throughout the World* (London, 1970). For a broader view of the period, attacks on the sporting calendar, and insights into other aspect of the conflict over play, there is the excellent Christopher Hill, *Society and Puritanism in Pre-Revolutionary England* (London, 1964).

Sporting Heraldry - the Rugby Union's Arms

3

Sport, Politeness and Profit

For the two centuries following the death of Charles II, his reign was to be looked back upon as a golden age for sport. The release from Puritan constraints meant that old recreations could revive and new forms of play take shape. The new freedoms, though, turned out to be far from complete. Some elements in the controlled life-style of the Commonwealth years made a continued appeal to law-makers and administrators, particularly those which contributed towards a regular working week and a more sober Sunday. Once the exuberance of the Restoration had subsided, however, a new attitude towards sport and recreation began to take over, marked by both a reasonable degree of toleration and an absence of much positive enthusiasm.

Popular festivities and games had their place again, though they were likely to be more hedged in than in the past. The rational minds of the eighteenth century could see sport as allowable to those in whom rational faculties were not fully developed, such as servants and children, or permissible to others by way of the occasional concession to human weakness. However, the search for profitable employment was constantly extending its boundaries and one of the commercial growth areas of the times came to be the exploitation of leisure. First in the world of entertainment, and then in sports and games, a new spirit of enterprise began to make its appearance. Paying spectators and paid players became a much more notable part of the sporting scene. Sporting crowds became larger and more frequent and then, as towns began to grow rapidly, looked upon with more suspicion. The second half of the eighteenth century saw the beginnings of modern sport. The fact that the social circumstances and the leisure calendar in which it had its birth were then to change dramatically would leave modern sport as a 'problem' for the Victorians to deal with.

The Maypoles Rise Again

In the summer of 1660, a Lancashire Puritan, Henry Newcombe, travelling to London, lamented the reappearance of maypoles and morris dancers, the first he had seen for twenty years: 'it is a sad sign the hearts of the people are poorly employed when they can make a business of playing the fool as they do.' The sights, and Newcombe's comments, are symptoms of the underlying tensions that were to surround popular play for many generations to come.

For the moment, in the 1660s, it was the spirit of release that was given free rein. The Saint's days were restored, less generously perhaps, but even the continental Catholics had drastically reduced the number to be observed. Parish feasts were often revived after what was in some cases fifty years of suspension, and where they did so they tended to expand into half a week or more of sport and celebration, to the growing annoyance of employers. The absence of restrictive legislation and consequent prosecutions makes it difficult to estimate the extent to which rural recreation flourished in these Restoration years, but it can be assumed that much of the old play was revived where it was not hampered by the enclosure of local playing grounds or residual local Puritan sentiment. The broad impression is that the old pursuits tended to coarsen as they moved further and further away from any ritualistic significance. The baiting and fighting of animals became more conspicuous and cock-fighting flourished across all social classes, having been one of the few sports which, on a small scale at least, Commonwealth governments had tolerated. Some of the older May games, too, tended to coarsen, developing cruder forms of the old courtship carnality of the chase into the woods. Women were 'heaved' or 'bumped' in several of those recorded - they became inclined to remain at home, according to one early report,' except those of less scrupulous character.'

But this was only one side of the coin. More acceptable games survived, and new ones began to be prominent. Edward Chamberlayne, writing in the 1660s, commented that for 'variety of divertisements, sports and recreations no nation doth exceed the English,' and went on to list those common among the 'citizens and peasants.' They included 'handball, football, skittles or ninepins, shovel board, goffe, troll-madam, cudgels, bear-baiting, bull-baiting, bow and arrow, throwing at cocks, shuttle-cock, bowling, quoits, leaping wrestling, pitching the bar and ringing of bells.' (Troll-madam was a game in which small balls were rolled into holes, usually nine of them, cut into a plank laid on edge. A later version of the game, Mississippi Tables, became a popular vehicle for gambling at race meetings - the scale was reduced and it was played on an easily portable board.)

Chamberlayne's list is an interesting one, both for its contents and its omissions. Neither cricket nor stoolball appear, for instance, though they were certainly being played in some parts of the country, with cricket already attracting sufficient crowds to justify an application for a beer licence. 'Skittles', 'ninepins' and 'bowls' had by now become clearly differentiated into separate games, while the appearance of 'goffe' is surprising as there is little other indication that the game was played south of the border other than by emigré Scots for another century and a half. Chamberlayne noted that bell-ringing was a sport 'used in no other country of the world,' perhaps becoming play by way of reaction against the Commonwealth prohibitions. It certainly remained so for many years, with reports of bell-ringing feats often appearing in the sporting press!

In spite of all this play activity, there were still limitations on popular sport and, so far as these were class-based, they were steadily strengthened rather than relaxed. New game laws fiercely protected the sporting rights of the larger landowners, with the 1671 Act forbidding even freeholders from killing game on their own land unless they were worth £100 a year or more. The royal hunting rights at Newmarket (where the heath had been ploughed during the Commonwealth to prevent racing) were even more jealously guarded. A 1663 proclamation forbade all hunting within seven miles of the town by other than the King's hounds, and banned the keeping of any greyhounds within ten miles. Newmarket, though, was becoming more and more a centre for racing rather than hunting during Charles II's reign. What had been set up as a hunting lodge by James I now saw the first relatively organised regular horse-racing. Charles would spend weeks there during the season - much to the discomfort of Pepys, who had to make trips there on official business. Mornings were spent at the cock-pit and the afternoons on the heath. The races were mostly matches for stakes, but there began to be more races for more than two horses. The Newmarket Town Plate was established by the King himself and the rules for this, and other later Royal Plates, were laid down and published 'at his Majesty's command.' Other race meetings began to achieve both social and sporting notice, particularly Epsom, where the King was again often present, but already Newmarket, from the concentration of horses kept there and the frequency of its events, was the centre of the sport. Towards the end of the century William III maintained the royal connection as a regular visitor and matchmaker.

Newmarket was exclusive. Another activity which looks back to Charles II for its first written rules - bowls - was much less class-bound. The King himself played on the Piccadilly Green and also had a green laid down at Windsor Castle. The rules were drawn up by Charles, his brother James, and the Duke of Buckingham (he of the palace), and envisage a game played by several players a side. They were remarkable among early sporting rules for their limited references to gambling, which was to be the main preoccupation of most eighteenth-century codes. The only gaming reference is in the rule forbidding bowlers or 'bettors' from interfering with a bowl 'by wind, hat, foot, or otherwise,' at the cost of losing the head. There is no doubt that bowls was a gambling game, with the alley described by Charles Cotton in his *Complete Gamester* as a 'place where three things are thrown away besides the bowls, viz: time, money, and curses, and the last ten for one.' It was already a game, to judge from Cotton's comments, where a skilled player (and deceptive matchmaker) could make a living for himself, and the same applied to both billiards and tennis. The latter was yet another sport favoured by Charles II, though his main interest seems to have been in seeing how profusely he sweated during play, being weighed before and after.

While there was progress on most sporting fronts, some activities did go into decline. Professional swordplay still attracted its crowds in London, but the sport tended to become something of a wild bloodbath, and singlestick contests began to take over, particularly as a fairground sport. Wrestling likewise retreated to its western heartlands, to Devon, Cornwall, and the Lake District, after professional roguery and intrigue undermined its attraction to London spectators - not the last time it would happen to that particular sport!

The practice of making money from sport was becoming much more common. Most of these late seventeenth-century professionals were freelance players operating on their own accounts, but already the paid professional began to make his appearance. Footmen were being employed for their speed, their masters making matches between their respective runners. Athletic contests became more frequent, often associated with festivals or fairs, and soon as additional attractions at race meetings or cricket matches. Attracting spectators did, indeed, become a much more frequent motive in the mounting of sporting events after the Restoration. While the vast majority of all play took place for pleasure, either its own or that involved in the stakes, there were more and more would-be entrepreneurs seeking to make profits from organised play. At this early stage, the usual means was by the selling of food and drink to spectators, with, for instance the Maidstone justices dealing in 1668 with an application to sell beer at cricket matches, while mine host of the Ram Inn, Smithfield, was being rated for a cricket field.

Cricket was one of the games making conspicuous progress, though it was still confined to the south-east of England. Its homeland was in the villages of Kent, Surrey, and Sussex, and it was also well-known in London. Teams still varied as to numbers, defined by local agreement, but there was clearly a broad consensus over how the game should be played, enough to make competition possible. London newspapers began to carry advertisements for games - there was to be cricket on Clapham Common on Easter Monday, 1700, for example, with no less than five games planned, indicating small sides or low scores! There are the first signs, too, of the aristocratic involvement that was to be so important in the future development of the game, with the Earl of Sussex spending £3 to go to a cricket match.

If cricket was achieving a degree of uniformity, the same could not be said of football, which retained all its local diversities. The mass communal struggles, suppressed during the interregnum, revived in force, though they began to live less easily in the towns. There were certainly, too, more restrained forms of football, though it is hard to estimate how widespread these were. The hurling match watched by Cromwell in Hyde Park had been played by no less than 159 Cornishmen, but clearly there was also play on a much smaller scale. The street football described by one French visitor to London as 'un exercise utile et charmant' can hardly have involved such hordes, and Roger North described how, after milking time, the dairy men on the family farm in Cambridgeshire would play football. The numbers may have been relatively few, but it was still too rough a game for the boys, who usually joined the maids in 'stoolball and such running games as they knew.' The boyhood football recalled by North may well have been influenced by the eastern counties variant of the game known as 'Camp' or 'Camping.' Here the number of players on each side was restricted and the ball had to be thrown, not passed hand to hand in scrimmages. The same name was given to the annual Shrove Tuesday game at Dorking, but here as elsewhere the traditional contest was an occasion for putting up the strongest shutters, keeping them tightly closed, and keeping off the streets!

There is little indication of the style of football being played in Scotland, but much evidence of its popularity. The habit was so ingrained among Edinburgh students that attempts at suppression were still needed as late as 1658, after nearly twenty years of parliamentary rule. There are several records of Scottish ministers finding the game so popular that it invaded the Sabbath, and they tried various means to stop it. John Ross of Blairgowrie, a cleric 'of unwonted muscular strength,' joined in the game one Sunday and hacked about so fiercely that soon all the other players were driven from the field. Welsh football could be both organised and bibulous. One Christmas Day game between two Cardiganshire villages was enlivened by an hour-long half-time beer drinking for both players and spectators, a celebration which doubtless accounted for the unruliness of the second half, when the players fell to 'fighting like bull-dogs.'

It was in Ireland that the game may have acquired by this time its most controlled form, with set pitches, more or less delineated as to their boundaries, and goals made of bent willow branches to form a hoop or gate. Behaviour was regulated at least to the extent that any man accused of foul play had to settle the issue after the match by wrestling his accuser. The original Irish game, like the Cornish, was played with a small ball, and it was clearly different from that played in England since teams were sometimes accused by opponents of copying the style of the English settlers. Irish football seems to have enjoyed a degree of order and regulation beyond what was found in the rest of Britain, with crowds watching the games and other supporting events on offer, such as 'dancing for cakes' by maidens.

All in all, the Restoration heralded a new richness and diversity in Britain's sport. Old play revived and new activities appeared. The introduction of metal skates from Holland, where the exiled court had discovered them, combined with a series of cold winters to give a boost to ice skating. Again at the exclusive level of the court, yacht racing began. Archery, freed now from any pretence of military training, began to revive mildly as a sport, particularly in Scotland, where, however, the Royal Company of Scottish Archers, founded in 1703, was an undercover Jacobite organisation, a military organisation masquerading as a sporting club! Hockey was being promoted by a Surrey publican in the 1660s and fives playing against church walls was already troubling churchwardens, particularly in the West Country.

The Puritan years, though, had left their lingering doubts over the nature and timing of popular recreation. Economic and social factors brought added force to piety in the urge to establish a tighter labour and leisure calendar. The thoroughly Cavalier parliaments of the Restoration proved no less zealous than their predecessors earlier in the century in seeking to legislate further against secular activities on the Sabbath. The eventual consequence was the Sunday Observance Act of 1677 to limit Sunday trading and travel. It had little immediate bearing on Sunday sport (unless the ban on people 'following their ordinary calling' on the Sabbath were to be applied to professional players) but it was indicative of a mood which was to make sport on the one assured day of popular freedom from work subject to doubt and interference. The underlying tone of the Restoration and of the Revolution Settlement of 1688 was one of restraint and moderation, once the original heady froth had been blown away. They were the heralds of a coming reasonable age, and reason tends to have little enthusiasm for anything but its own workings. Certainly not for play.

Sport and the Rational Man
Competitive play demands eagerness, fervour, a suspension of disbelief. Whatever its conscious, cognitive elements, its home lies in the emotions and in the spirit. Matching an often irrelevant form of prowess against that of another human being, striving, winning or losing - these are its essence. There have been heroic ages in human history, such as Homeric Greece or Elizabethan England, when such endeavouring matched the spirit of the times. There have been other epochs when they did not, and the British eighteenth century was certainly one of these.

After the Glorious Revolution and the peaceful succession of the Hanoverians, the country felt itself safe from both despotism and Catholicism, its twin anathemas of the previous century. The advance of knowledge had provided a satisfactory explanation of the whole universe, showing this to be a rational world presided over by an equally rational deity. Reason was all, moderation was the key, and restraint in all things the recipe for the good life in a polite society. Enthusiasm was a pejorative word, and sport was to find its place usually in the margins of serious consideration. The prevailing attitude still owed much to Puritanism, stripped of most of its spiritual component but also of most of its repression. The prevalent mood was one of usually benign national neglect, in which sport found space to grow with a perhaps surprising vigour.

The church played less and less of a part in the country's recreational life, either by way of promotion or prevention. Many eighteenth-century clergy were preoccupied with furthering their own social status and, with Whigs in apparently permanent power in both church and state, many country parsons were disposed to join the local Tory squire, whooping to the hunt with the hounds. They acquiesced in the old popular play of the parish rather than either promoting or quashing it. Various societies for the 'Reformation of Manners' rose to spasmodic prominence at times during the century, and the manners that gave offence were usually those associated with the people's play. When John Wesley began to preach to the lower orders, it was to save their souls not to promote behaviour which seemed inappropriate for an enlightened age. Popular recreation, particularly the traditional pursuits rooted in the past, had to face steady pressure from several quarters, but as the old was gradually hedged in, the new found room to grow.

The old communal play too often seemed to be a reminder of less civilised ages. Its spiritual opponents were powerfully reinforced by its secular critics, who came to see 'Idleness' (as distinct from the 'leisure' of the wealthy) as one of the rising sins of the times. An anonymous cleric set the tone in 1766 when he remarked that 'the lesser time for idleness any trade allowed, the better it was.' It was a sentiment which became widely shared, particularly by employers like Josiah Wedgwood, who found his potters wandering off from wake to wake throughout the summer months. As first water power and then, at the end of the century, steam power brought more mechanised production and higher capital investment, the demand for regular working hours became all the more insistent. Expensive plant had to be used to the full. It was a gradual and patchy process - factory production was virtually unknown in Birmingham until the second half of the next century - but the move towards the reduction of the workers' holidays was already irrevocably tied to the growth of industrialisation.

Furthermore, all the long-standing suspicions of popular leisure remained. Holidays meant sport. Sport brought large numbers together - larger than ever as populations grew and became more concentrated in towns. Large gatherings meant rowdiness, tumult, or worse. Arranging football matches to attract enough of the disaffected to pull down enclosure fences, stop fen drainage, or demolish mills, was not unknown - it happened on at least three occasions in the middle years of the century in the Eastern counties. Such incidences of out-and-out rioting might be rare, but they could only add to the overall distrust. Even if there was nothing intrinsically wrong with playing cricket, rowing boats, or racing horses, to quote just the more acceptable current sporting pursuits, there were always doubts about the settings in which they took place, their mass attraction, the gambling, and the disreputable company which seemed to be their inevitable components.

On the other hand, wholesale suppression was against the mood of the times. Popular sport might have to yield to the property interests of the enclosing landlord, to the restrictiveness of the game laws, and it might have its conflicts with employers seeking to impose regular work patterns or with Sabbatarians trying to impose a quieter Sunday, yet it suffered little disturbance on any national scale. There was virtually no legislation passed in restraint of play: a statute of Queen Anne's restricting the level of gambling stakes was a dead letter virtually from the start; the 1740 Act designed to limit the unrestricted growth of horse-racing by demanding prizes of at least £50 for each race had little practical effect; and the 1780 Sunday Observance Act forbidding the opening of places of entertainment which charged for entrance was never conceived with sport in mind and only became relevant to sport in the next century and later.

People of all classes were determined to have both their quota of leisure and to enjoy it without overmuch impediment. If there should be some squeezing in of leisure, all the more reason to enjoy to the full that which was granted. With a free spirit of enterprise in the air, what could be more natural than the appearance of new promoters and providers to meet this demand. If one effect of the growing use of capital was to reduce leisure time, another was to open up more and more opportunities for the commercial exploitation of that leisure.

The Pounds and the Pennies
Any eighteenth-century town of any pretence soon came to have its theatre. In the cities there were circuses, often resident. There were lending libraries, music concerts, and a local press which carried the advertisements of the amusements on offer. Equally, there came to be provision for sport, both active and passive. There were swimming baths - one in Birmingham was 100 ft by 30ft, and charged 1/- entrance in 1787 - riding schools, fencing academies, lessons in the pugilistic art, and boats for hire. The London apprentices would take over fifty cutters out on the Thames on Sundays. Many sporting events were widely publicised to bring in the spectators - cricket matches, horse-racing, foot races and cocking matches, and even prize-fights in the first half of the century, before they became nominally illegal.

That time-honoured free-enterprise provider of sporting fare, the publican, became ever more resourceful in catering for his customers' zest for amusement. Inside, there were parlour games, skittles, often cock- and dog-fighting. Outside, there was bowls, cricket and horse-racing if he had a field, and duck-hunting with dogs if he had a pond. Even the publican, though, could be drawn into the new larger-scale capitalism. Brewing was one of the earliest industries to become mechanised and the Whitbreads, already the owners of numerous London taverns, were showing off their new steam engine to the King and Queen before the century was out. The publican, too, had to face much more rivalry than in the past.

Conspicuous sporting events had, by and large, depended on patronage. This mode of support continued to be of primary importance and cricket in particular benefited from the involvement and investment of noble players, who made the matches (often for one thousand guineas stakes), provided the grounds

A more enclosed and controlled venue for a prizefight than was usually feasible once the sport had become outlawed. This was Richard Humphries v. Daniel Mendoza in 1798.

and equipment, and paid (or employed) the professional players. Names such as the Earl of Dorset, Lord Winchelsea and Sir Thomas Mann figure prominently in the game's early history. Much the same patronage supported the rise of pugilism, though here the patrons were backers and promoters, not competitors themselves, and many of these, such as the Duke of Hamilton, the Honourable Charles Wyndham and Sir Watkin Williams Wynn, were also notable racehorse owners.

Corporate, as well as individual patronage, was also well established. The numerous Royal Plates did much to promote the turf at favoured courses from the mid-eighteenth century through to the nineteenth, while local town corporations often gave active financial backing to their race meetings, investing in grandstands and general improvements. The motives were clearly commercial, attracting visitors and business, as well as sporting, as they were in the case of the race funds raised by local subscription, when the charges levied on stall holders and other beneficiaries from the meeting were always considerably higher for outsiders than for the patrons.

Entrance fees from spectators played only a small part in the overall financing of sport at this stage, largely because enclosed playing areas were unusual. Advantageous viewpoints, such as grandstands at racecourses (which only became 'grand' in any recognisable sense late in the century) or the ex-pugilists' wagons at fights, could always demand a charge, but a free sight of races was always available and attempts to collect entrance monies at fights were haphazard and often unsuccessful. It was the other needs of spectators which offered profit - their food, drink, travel and accommodation, and the temptations of the gaming tables, the playing cards and the dice. The ground rents to be charged for booths and stalls at race meetings were critical to their success, and were set out comprehensively in all advertisements - they had to fit the market and the quality of sport on offer, and there is evidence that overcharging played its part in the frequent failures of eighteenth-century racing ventures, many of which were short-lived.

Money matters exerted a growing influence on the nature and organisation of sport. The best players were in increasing demand. Promoters wanted them because they would attract the crowds. They were sought by backers, by cricket captains and racehorse owners to defend the stake money, and wealthy patrons sustained the practice of taking the best performers into their permanent employment. By the end of the century, however, the freelance professional was as common as the hired man. Patrons found that cricketers did not necessarily make good gamekeepers and if, like Aylward, they were given the catering rights in Sir Thomas Mann's home games, their performance was always likely to bear evidence of the fact! Pugilists did continue into the Regency years to be employed as 'minders' by some of the more raffish members of the nobility, and the groom-cum-jockey still trailed his master's racehorse from one country meeting to another, often for much of the summer, but the trend was towards a much more contractual relationship between employer and employed. The professional cricketer began to be paid by the match (£5 a day, plus expenses, was common), while professional jockeys came to be independent suppliers of their services to the highest bidder, a process hastened by the move towards the end of the century to shorter races run by younger horses. These were given light weights to carry, limits to which no decently portly gentleman of the period could think it proper to reduce himself.

It seldom meant any life-long prosperity for the professional sportsman. A few moved into other occupations with success. Richard Humphries, the boxing champion of the 90s, built up a flourishing coal merchant's business near the present site of the Savoy Hotel, and some others, like that earlier champion, Jack Broughton, enjoyed a long and decent life on the basis of their sporting profits. More typical, though, was the fate of Humphries' great rival, Dan Mendoza, who spent the rest of his life hovering on the fringes of the ring, trying his hand with little real success at any number of enterprises, including tavern-keeping, eventually dying in poverty. One Victorian boxing historian aptly remarked that your pugilist is no more than a publican in embryo, but it was an occupation for which many of them were little suited, drinking away their winnings or rotting their livers. Cricketers sometimes moved into the same profession, and sometimes with the same sad fate. One of them, Noah Mann (on no account to be confused with the noble Sir Thomas!) was burnt to death, asleep before his own ale-house fire after carousing with his cronies, 'a victim of his own intemperance,' according to his obituary. Jockeys could, by and large, fare slightly better. The turf offered a wide range of employments other than riding, careers could be lengthy, and there were families such as the Days with several generations of

James Figg's handbill advertising his boxing emporium in the sport's legal days. Advertisement of sport is as old as paid spectating.

successful employment behind them who were able to rise to an independence which rivalled that of some of their former employers. The life of the professional sportsman, however, remained for most a precarious one. He might have gold jingling his pockets from bets and tips after a big win, but defeat could be disastrous. There are many reports of half-conscious pugilists being thrown into a carriage and left there helpless while their backers went off to watch the following bouts.

Apart from the immediate financial rewards of the contest itself, there was considerable ancillary commercial involvement. Racing, in particular, had become a business, especially at Newmarket and at some of the grand stables built at great country houses. The permanent establishments of the owners at Newmarket cost money and brought employment. They meant not only expenditure on tack and equipment, stud fees, proceeds from sales, and a general rush of business during the half dozen or so race weeks, but also spasmodic bursts of prosperity for all the horse-changing inns on the road from London. Money flowed back and forth, spelling profit for some, but ruination for many a family fortune.

One consequence of the heavy investment in sport was the need for regulation. Agreed methods of proceeding and competing were essential if contests were to take place at all with any reliability. At the simplest level, the

West Country poet, William Barnes, tells the tale of the Dorset cudgel player being surprised when the Devon wrestler dived at his ankles! This, though, was only the beginning. Large sums at risk in wagers meant that the terms of competition had to be based on something more precise than inherited custom. The need expressed itself during a great age of codification, with Blackstone producing his *Commentaries of the Laws of England*, and it was a fitting moment for the rules of sport to begin to take on a firmer form. These rules combined two strands, the one inherited from concepts of honour, as old as the days of chivalry, the other depending very much on the law of contract, the contract involved in the wager.

It was where the investment was greatest that the rules first felt the need to be comprehensive. The 'Rules Concerning Horse Racing in General' were well established by the time they appeared in the first *Racing Calendars* in the middle of the century. They were supplemented by the 'Rules and Orders of the Jockey Club' (designed simply for Newmarket, but widely referred to elsewhere) and by the 'Articles' specific to King's Plates, derived from those originally laid down in Charles II's reign. Broadly speaking, some threequarters of these rules defined not the racing itself, but the terms for betting on it. The first cricket code appeared in 1727 and the laws of the game went through periodic re-draftings from 1744 onwards. They, likewise, gave consideration to the terms of wagers on the game, and continued to do so as late as their 1830 version, while individual matches often had their own 'articles' or contracts, which laid down specific requirements, particularly as to the number of professionals to be brought into each side and similar conditions. Major fights were also usually governed by such individual contracts which amplified the limited demands of the rules themselves, and which give the most striking example of this stress on the betting element. Jack Broughton's original rules for pugilistic contests had just one sentence defining when and where a man could be hit - above the waist, when on his feet - with all the remainder of the rules concerned with the wagering on the fight and the procedures to be followed. As with all the other codes, too, they were originally purely local in intention. The racing regulations were for Newmarket, the cricket rules were designed for what became the MCC, and Broughton's were solely for his own amphitheatre. They became national rules with varying degrees of rapidity, as other clubs and match-makers found them convenient or, as with the Jockey Club, they were denied arbitration on disputes unless they followed its rules. But this was to belong to the next century.

While much of the prevailing moral and economic climate of the eighteenth century might appear inimical to both leisure and its sporting employment, these were bolstered by the commercial undercurrent which flowed with the persistent human search for competitive entertainment. Through this, and the exercise of privilege by wealthy patrons, recognisably modern forms of individual and team competition took shape, and both the sporting calendar and the sporting map became significant elements in the nation's sporting life.

Sporting Places and Sporting Times

In the eighteenth century, for the first time, sport began to take on nation-wide characteristics. No longer were organised sporting events relatively occasional and unconnected highlights of the recreational scene. They began to build up into a regular pattern of codified play and, as part of the process, they increasingly broke away from their traditional holiday occasions and began to establish their own claims for sporting life.

The earliest of the competitive spectator sports, horse-racing, was the most organised, the most integrated, and the most extensive. With meetings in all four countries, virtually all the population could get to a racecourse at least once a year. By their very ubiquity, the races attracted more spectators than any other major sporting events, though, paradoxically, at racing's unchallenged head-quarters, Newmarket, spectators were both few and thoroughly discouraged. Racing took place on courses scattered all over the heath, and was impossible to follow on foot. It was a place for the gentry owners and backers, and even their own ladies were left at home.

There were some half dozen weeks of racing annually. The cards would be full for the first three or four days. They would begin to peter out by Friday and only occasionally was there any racing by Saturday. A typical day's racing was that of the Monday of the 1773 First Spring Meeting, when there were four sweepstakes (the first of which had two dukes and five others with titles among the owners) and seven two-horse matches. Over 3,000 guineas changed hands, either in stake money or forfeits.

It was common practice for the more enthusiastic followers to actually gallop alongside the racing horses. While this was feasible at Newmarket, it was highly dangerous at other meetings, where the picture was very different, in both social and sporting terms. The local races came just once a year, and for the people they meant a break from work, whether formally granted or not. For the county they were grand occasions, an opportunity for the gentry to stay in town for a few days, or to entertain if they lived nearby. The participation of the ladies was actively encouraged, they would watch the sport from their carriages and often contributed to a 'Ladies' Plate' for one of the races. The highlight of the week (so it was called, though the racing seldom covered more than two days) was the Race Ball on the last night, but there were usually assemblies, plays, and concerts to go to as well.

Descriptions of these race days are always full of colour and excitement. The whole town would be agog as folk flocked in from the villages, and on the course there would be a bustling crowd thronging round the drink sellers, the sweetmeat stalls, the sideshows, and the gambling tables. Moralists were quick to point out that others were also attracted there - the light-fingered pickpocket, the trickster, and the prostitute. The actual racing, though, could be the least of it. Meetings were usually held on midweek days, one reason being the hope of attracting horses (some of them from Newmarket) which spent the weekends being walked from course to course, but fields still often remained small, with no more than half a dozen horses running in the whole meeting. They made up for it by running races in heats, usually three or four miles each, and it was not unusual for a horse to run on two successive days. They were obviously contests of stamina rather than speed, and tight finishes were something of a rarity.

Such meetings covered the country, well over sixty of them in 1787, from Penrith in the far north to St Ives in Cornwall. The *Racing Calendar* for the same year reported six meetings in Scotland and four in Wales, while Ireland had its own version of Newmarket at The Curragh. Here there were four full weeks of racing in 1773, for instance, and at least fifteen other Irish meetings in the same year.

Racing was in advance of all other sports in both its spread and its comparative regularity. While local meetings could have their oddities, and few went off without some complaint or other, there was generally the odd racing man about who had some experience of the sport at its leading edge, even before the Jockey Club became the customary arbiter over objections. Cricket, however, was much more limited geographically. In spite of occasional references to such bizarre happenings as cricket on the frozen River Tyne at Newcastle in 1776, it was essentially still a game of London and the South-East, with some flourishing pockets in the Midlands, its period of national expansion not beginning in earnest until the early years of the next century. The progress of the game in this century was none the less remarkable. From being a country game, largely confined to Wealden villages and their neighbouring towns, it came to have such sophisticated features as written rules, umpires, specialised venues, paying spectators and paid professional players. London came to be particularly well served, with cricket being played at White Conduit Fields, Chertsey, Richmond Green, Croydon, and Walworth and Clapham Commons. Above all, there was the Artillery Ground, the site of most of the big matches in the capital, and such a magnet to the crowds in the middle of the century that magistrates were called upon to suppress the 'increasing evil' it was alleged to encourage.

While it only cost two-pence to watch the cricket at the Artillery Ground, it was only the stern-minded who could have a cheap day there. Apart from drinking the proprietor's ales - for they were publicans first, and sports promoters only second - there was constant temptation to bet on the play. Gambling was as inherent in cricket as in racing, and with matches themselves known to have up to £1,000 depending on the result, betting fever spread readily around the ground. With so much financial interest on the result among the spectators, interference with the play was not uncommon, to the rising annoyance of the aristocratic leaders of the game. In a move that foreshadowed the present 'remedy' for football disorder, they forced the proprietor in 1744 to provide bench seats and triple his prices - with the result that attendances fell at once from 7,000 a day to under 200. It was not long before the old prices were restored.

Going to play cricket in the Midlands could be even more hazardous. While most matches seem to have been fairly peaceable, fierce local rivalries could always boil over into violence, an outcome made all the more likely by the absence of large-scale gentry participation, uncertainty over rules, and the inexperience of umpires. After one game in 1787 between Leicester and Coventry, there was a pitched battle in Hinkley, where the visitors were refreshing themselves, and there followed what one local reporter called 'a scene of bloodshed scarcely to be credited in a country so entirely distinguished for acts of humanity.' The antagonism aroused here came in part from the feeling that this was in essence a county contest between Leicestershire and Warwickshire, and gave a ready opportunity for the expression of county rivalries. The county, indeed, began to be an important entity in sporting organisation - eventually becoming so strong as to defy, on the cricket field, the local government changes. County competition first showed itself in a sport with no long-term organised future, namely cock-fighting. Matches between the 'Gentlemen' of one county and those of another were widespread, frequent, and were often advertised as 'annual' fixtures, the first instance of a regular programme of team contests in any sport. Like county cricket later, these cock matches were usually three-day events, and often associated with race meetings. The reason for the importance of the county in the development of organised sport are well worth further exploration, starting doubtless from the fact that, outside the corporate towns, the county was the one substantial administrative body in existence and the quarterly meeting of its justices brought together those most likely to prove its sporting innovators.

As sport became more regular, it began to settle into its own calendar patterns. Cricket matches, for instance, favoured the early part of the week, and usually avoided the weekend. Prize-fighting came to concentrate on Mondays and Tuesdays, the emphasis moving to the latter in the early years of the next century.

Locally, the combat sports made steady progress through the eighteenth century, with cudgel play gradually giving way to boxing or, in some areas, wrestling. Some Wessex counties were the exception. There, cudgelling and singlestick fighting remained the usual human fighting sports throughout the period. Elsewhere, the style of boxing codified by Jack Broughton became the vogue. In the mid-century, pugilism enjoyed a brief period of legal acceptance and noble support, centred on Broughton's own sporting theatre in the Oxford Road, a flourishing (and expensive) venue for regular contests. This all came to an end when Broughton lost a fight unexpectedly as a result of a chance blow, and his prime patron, the Duke of Cumberland (the 'Butcher' of Culloden) lost £10,000. The odds at which the bet was made - ten to one - were farcical, but this did not save Broughton, or his sport. Pugilism was driven more or less underground, though it did return to royal favour and begin to enjoy its golden age in the last decade of the century.

Still illegal then, and occasionally subject to prosecutions (always of the pugs themselves, never their organisers and still less their backers), prize-fights could attract enormous crowds, particularly as they were drawn from a population one tenth of today's. 10,000 was not unusual. Curiosity about the doings of the famous boxers - Humphries, Dan Mendoza, Gentleman John Jackson and, later, the Belchers and Tom Cribb, made them the first national sporting heroes. Boxing was, indeed, a nation-wide sport with pugilists coming from all four home countries - national loyalties were often stressed (and even exaggerated) as part of the build-up towards fights. Ireland, and the highly successful Bristol area, were the main nurseries for prize-fighters, but wherever a man came from he could only achieve fame through the London ring. Fights were arranged at one of the succession of London taverns which were the unofficial headquarters of the sport, and they were usually held within riding distance of the capital. The exceptions were mainly for contests arranged to coincide with racing interests, which could take them to venues such as Doncaster, Newmarket, or the West Midlands.

The money staked on boxing matches was often rivalled, and sometimes exceeded, by that involved in pedestrianism, the period's form of athletics. This was another of the sports which drew in the crowds all over the kingdom. There were races run at festivals and fairs everywhere, and some even enlivened other sporting events such as cricket matches. Matches between athletic ladies tended to be especially well advertised and reported, their flimsy attire being seen as an added attraction to male spectators. The most conspicuous pedestrian feats, though, were usually performed against the clock or the calendar, with races forming only a minority of those contests which attracted large sums of money. Long distance events were the most noted aspect of the sport, and the trip from

London to York and back became as famous a record as the 1500 metres is today. Foster Powell achieved the feat in six days in 1773, and before the turn of the century three other challengers had in turn brought the time down to 5 days 14½ hours. The contenders could be, in effect, professionals, or gentlemen backing their own performance - 1,000 guineas, for instance, on a walk between London and Guildford in 7½ hours - and there were athletic oddities which could take pedestrianism nearer to the circus ring than the athletic track. One wager for 1,000 guineas made between a duke and a baronet in 1793 (such coyness was usual in sporting reports) was for covering 10 miles in 3 hours, *taking 4 steps forward and one back*! It was the precursor of even stranger and more eccentric spectacles, which would involve trundling wheelbarrows, hopping, bowling hoops, picking up potatoes, and all manner of other challenges.

Pedestrian contests, both conventional and freakish, were among the first spectator events to make their appearance in the growing industrial towns - they were easy to set up, needing few facilities, and their promoters were the most alert of the new sport entrepreneurs. They were alive to the new thirst for sensation, for novel sporting entertainment. Symptomatic of this was the rapid development of boating races in the last two decades of the century. Rowing matches between professional watermen were doubtless as old as the trade itself, and they had been formalised on the River Thames in the annual race for Doggett's Coat and Badge, first rowed for in 1717. Nor were sailing races a complete novelty - they had taken place with Charles II - but both forms of water competition suddenly became matters of frequent interest and enthusiasm. By the 1790s there were frequent races, rowing and sailing, on the Thames, and any number of private matches. The Cumberland Society, the earliest sailing club, had already set out rules for racing and was arbitrating over disputes, while the new sports were spreading rapidly. Sea racing took place along the coast, in such places as Bradwell, in Essex, which had its prize silver cup, while village festivals where water was at hand began to include boating races of greater or less seriousness. All reports speak of thousands flocking to the river banks or the sea shore whenever races were announced.

Other sports, less widespread or less catholic in their appeal, could draw their crowds. Wrestling might have largely retreated to the Celtic fringes of England, where it was always popular, and was a frequent accompaniment to local race meetings. There were occasional bouts by visiting wrestlers in London, and some scattered reports of competitions elsewhere - even to a crowd of 10,000 in Bedfordshire in 1737. Coursing hares with greyhounds was an ancient sport, and while it was socially exclusive and a sport for dog owners rather than spectators, it did become much more organised on a competitive basis in the last quarter of the century, with numerous meetings all over the country, all of them fully covered by the sporting press. There was also a revival of archery, now avowedly a sport with no pretence at military usefulness. The *Sporting Magazine* in 1793 listed twenty of 'the principal societies or companies of archers' (implying that there were others) often with such exotic titles as the Hainault Foresters and the Robin Hood Bowmen. Even pigeon-racing had started and had its own association, the Columbarian Society, which arranged sweepstakes of £40 each among its members. The pigeons often covered the flight from Newmarket to London in less than three hours, which suggests another, and possibly less honest, sporting possibility in their use.

The several sided relationship between sport and morality was one that would be increasingly scrutinised as society itself began to take on a new seriousness. It would do so, though, against a sporting panorama which had begun to cover all the kingdom and in the face of sporting activities which had asserted their rights to *time*, especially on Mondays or Tuesdays. Little that was totally new was still to make its appearance on the sporting scene. Its subsequent story would be one of facing trials and vicissitudes from both without and within before a fully modern sporting world could emerge from the embryo a century later.

The Living Past III

Many sporting venues from this period are still readily identifiable. Those still in use for their original activities are much rarer, confined almost entirely to a handful of bowling greens and rather more racecourses. The greens, such as those at Christchurch and Bedford Priory, were often of medieval origin, on sites which were protected from subsequent development. Extant racecourses tended to survive through their siting on common land or sustained sponsorship. Epsom, Ascot, Doncaster, Worcester, Warwick, and, of course, Newmarket, are among those still in their original locations.

Even more intriguing is the search for traces of the numerous racecourses in use during the eighteenth century (and later). The *Sporting Magazine*, in 1798, had a list of 49 race meetings 'dropped within fifty years past,' and even that is far from complete. It includes, for instance, Spalding, Newark, Barnstaple, Loughborough, Derby, Maidenhead, Wisbech, Bodmin, Cirencester, Barnet, Lancaster, Peterborough, Ipswich, Scarborough, Wakefield, Preston, and so on. In fact there were few towns of any size that did not, at some time, venture to launch a race meeting - and if they did not do so, even that is worth exploring. Indications of old racecourses may come from surviving names such as Racedown Farm (Blandford), or Racecourse Lane (Stourbridge, and elsewhere). Even modern maps can sometimes give clues, as subsequent building sometimes followed the existing shape of the course, or pathways may still do so. Street names often recall, too, old bowling places - in the Birmingham area, as well as in the city itself, they are found in Dudley, Hinkley, Stourbridge and Warwick, while there are half a dozen or more in London.

Once sport began to be commercialised and designed to cater for crowds, its sites were as near to the town centre as possible. Inevitably, as the town expanded, the venue was swallowed up. London, as by far the largest and the most precocious in its sporting development, provides the prime example. In the mid-eighteenth century the river was its southern boundary, Hyde Park was at its western edge, Oxford Street and Holborn had green fields lying to the north and the City faced open country to the east. It is around these fringes, in particular, that numerous traces of the sport of the period remain. The process of urbanisation began early. The Spring Garden at Charing Cross, a rural setting for bowls in the seventeenth century, was built over in Charles II's reign, its name surviving in the street just behind Whitehall. Just south of the river, Bankside disappeared as a bear garden at much the same time, but memories remain by Blackfriars Bridge - Bear Lane, Bull Alley, and that old Elizabethan baiting ground, Paris Garden. At the then north-eastern corner of the town, the present Clerkenwell, were a host of sporting places. There was Hockley in the Hole, rough and raffish, with its regular baiting and gambling taverns, until it

THE

Sporting Magazine

OR

MONTHLY CALENDAR

of the

TRANSACTIONS OF

THE TURF, THE CHACE,

And every other Diversion

Interesting to

The Man of Pleasure and Enterprize.

VOLUME THE FIRST.

LONDON.

Printed for the PROPRIETORS, and Sold by J. WHEBLE;

Nº 18. Warwick Square, Warwick Lane, near St Pauls.

MDCCXCIII.

Sporting Magazine - the title page of the first volume. Its appearance in 1793 marked the start of regular sporting journalism.

disappeared with drainage improvements in 1756. It was here that prize-fighting had begun its emergence from cudgel play and sword fighting as a separate sport. 'Perilous Pool,' long noted for its duck hunting, was converted into a 60 by 30 yard swimming bath in 1743, and is still marked by Peerless Street, near Old Street station. Then, just north of the Pentonville Road was White Conduit House, with a meadow beside it on which gentlemen began to play cricket - the ancestor of Lord's and the M.C.C. Hyde Park and St James's Park housed almost every type of sport at one time or another - pugilism, wrestling, foot races, football exhibitions, and so on.

Many more London examples could be quoted, and while the same richness can hardly be expected elsewhere, most towns will doubtless have something to tell of these early days of organised sport. More aids to the search come to hand in the eighteenth century, particularly in the widespread appearance of local newspapers, an invaluable source, and not just in their advertisements of matches and reports of events. Notices of the sale of inns, for instance, will sometimes reveal the existence of sporting facilities, such as bowling alleys or greens. Nationally, the *Racing Calendar* appeared annually from the 1740s, and it reveals much more about the sport than might at first appear - its finances, ownership, the movement of horses, the status of meetings, and much else.

By this period there is indeed a wealth of contemporary material, in print and in manuscript. For the latter, county record offices are a main source, with the advantage that diaries, letters, and documents are now likely to be more easily readable. Many published works have valuable sporting clues. To take just one example at random, Defoe's *A Tour through the Whole Island of Great Britain* (1724-26) has references to cheating at Newmarket, bowls at York, Banstead Races, horse breeding, racing at Nottingham, York, and Aylesbury, and summer evening sport at Epsom.

One of the best pictures of urban life is in Margaret George, *London Life in the Eighteenth Century* (London, 1925), available in later paperback editions. There is no overall sports history of the period, but Richard Holt's *Sport and the British: A Modern History* (Oxford, 1989) begins to come into its own and Robert W. Malcolmson, *Popular Recreation in English Society 1700-1850* (Cambridge, 1973) is excellent within its own terms, which do not give much emphasis to the new organised sport. The major sport to make its appearance at this time was pugilism and its overall rise and fall is surveyed in Dennis Brailsford, *Bareknuckles: A Social History of Prize-Fighting* (Cambridge, 1988). Its later Regency heyday is well described in John Ford, *Prizefighting: The Age of Regency Boximania* (Newton Abbot, 1971).

4

Sport in Smoke and Shadow

The later years of the eighteenth century and the first half of the nineteenth were difficult times for popular sport. Old habits had to cope with new circumstances. The long shift of productive labour from agriculture to industry began to get under way, and with it the move from the land to the town. Uneven as the process was, both in England and in the rest of the islands, its acute consequences in the burgeoning industrial towns of the north and the Midlands had their ripple effects on the whole population. Nor was it just a matter of material change. A new air of moral earnestness began to blow through the land, challenging the rational amorality that had characterised much of the past century's practice. By its end, Methodism had become a spiritual force to be reckoned with, and by the accession of Victoria the new seriousness was being firmly buttressed by a growing and influential body of evangelical clerics within the established church. None of them found the popular recreations of their day any more palatable than their Puritan forbears had in their times.

Both the old customary play, often coarsened and made all the more clamorous by the ever-bigger crowds, and the rowdy spectacles of the cock-pit, the racecourse, and the prize-ring faced opposition on all sides - from parsons who found them heathenish and evil, from landlords who saw crowds as a perpetual threat to property, and from employers looking always for more regular work schedules. The occasions for play were under threat from persistent pressures to enforce tighter labour disciplines, while its locations were often put at risk by the numerous enclosures of once open land.

It was an environment in which sport and recreation had to find new styles, new outlets, if it was to survive with any promise for the future. The fact that it did so, but often in modes no more acceptable than the old, in turn gave rise to concerns over the 'problem' of leisure. Purposeful minds questioned not only the availability of leisure opportunities, but also, as they looked around them, the proper recreational use of such free time as the people might be granted - or chose to take. Even as they did so, the whole sporting balance of the land began to change, its axis tilting ever more strongly towards the Midlands and the North. Henceforth the history of British sport would cease to be predominantly focused on the south-east of England.

The Encouragement of Piety and Virtue

The parish church of the past had been the pivot of the local recreational scene. Its calendar had provided the occasions, its precincts a frequent playground, and the cleric was usually a benign observer if not an active patron. The eighteenth-century English parson, however, gradually cut himself off from the communal life of his flock. Tithes were commuted, great rectories built, and the younger sons of the gentry began to see the church as a fit career. As his social status grew, his influence on his congregation all too often waned in proportion. His own sporting energies went increasingly to the hunt, the coursing field, and the shoot. Neglect rather than repression was the main feature of the church's attitude towards popular recreation, a neglect in which some festivities could survive with vigour, but which took away from others one prop against attack from other quarters.

The first official shot in the campaign for a stricter morality came from George III in 1787 with his proclamation 'For the Encouragement of Piety and Virtue, and for the Preventing or Punishing of Vice.' It was aimed at public sin, but the 'Proclamation Societies' which it inspired soon found themselves attacking the only definable sin they could identify - sabbath breaking. It was hardly the immorality of the poor that the King had most in mind, but they would have been the worst sufferers had the movement been successful, especially as their other opportunities for play were being hedged in. But more vigorous campaigns were on their way. Methodists and then, from within the Church of England, Evangelicals both looked to new modes of behaviour and became deeply suspicious of popular play, with its opportunities for waste, keeping bad company, and backsliding. Victorian morality was on the march well before the young Queen came to the throne - after all, the assiduous Dr Bowdler rooted out Shakespeare's indecencies as early as 1817 - and Methodists were banning all attendance at wakes and feasts in the 1820s. Soon reforming parsons were putting down old festivals, harassing local race meetings, and even stopping prize-fights.

While the main practical thrust of the new zeal was against the leisure pursuits of the masses, the upper-class had become sensitive to criticisms of its own role, particularly with revolutionary lessons from across the channel in mind. The landed gentry had no intention of depriving themselves of their own sporting pleasures, but they found it convenient to dissociate themselves gradually from popular sporting activities which they had once assiduously patronised. The advent of the professional cricketer, paid not by permanent employment but by match fees, relieved them of any long-term obligations, while in pedestrianism and pugilism disenchantment was encouraged by the falling honesty of contests from about 1820 onwards. It was a process which upper-class withdrawal only served to accelerate, since with it went the aristocratic code of fair play that honour bound the gentry to maintain.

As the age of the entrepreneur dawned, the upper-classes felt a growing need to demonstrate their own usefulness and even, at length, to identify themselves - so long as they did not compromise their own privileges - with the new middle-class morality. But they tended to remain apart, acquiescing in the dominant mood rather than embracing it enthusiastically. It showed in their sports, which became increasingly exclusive and self-contained. Symptomatically, the *Sporting Magazine*, which from its founding in 1792 had covered every imaginable sport

Squirrel Hunting and *Coursing the Bustard*, two etchings from *Sporting Magazine* (April 1799)

from walking to bell-ringing, and from cudgel play to cock-fighting, had, by the late 1830s, come to centre entirely on horses, dogs, and the killing of birds, beasts and fowl.

Hunting both flourished and became socially more restrictive. Chasing the fox, once thought unworthy prey, as vermin, became fashionable, and where foxes were not available they were imported - Scottish foxes were said, in 1823, to be better than French, since they were fitter and fatter! With most foxes kennelled and then released especially for the hunt, there were no spurious claims about ridding the countryside of pests. There were over forty packs listed in the press in the 1820s, while the old artisan 'hunts' (such as the Rochdale Weavers') were being faced with louder and louder disapproval for 'setting the whole country at defiance,' damaging woods and fences, and 'abusing their neighbours and benefactors.' Such comments became typical. As the wealthy became more exclusive in their own play, they joined more and more in the attacks on pursuits they had once accepted.

However, too stark an analysis of class divisions in sport, particularly in these times of change, runs the risk of over-simplification. If Victorianism had a protracted birth, the Regency spirit was in some quarters long to die. There were still dandies in the 1840s, and sportsmen of the old school survived well into the second half of the nineteenth century - characters such as Squire Osbaldeston, pan-athlete extraordinary, huntsman, runner, cricketer, oarsman, and shot, who, once his own active days were eventually over, carried on as promoter and arbiter. In the darkest days of the prize-ring there would still be young sprigs of the nobility in the crowds and as late as 1874 a clergyman could shock the respectable by revealing himself as the owner of the St Leger winner. Equally, to make the assumption that all members of the middle and commercial classes were opposed to sport is also wide of the mark. There were, for instance, always reputable tradesmen on hand to stand as sureties for any prize-fighters who might come before the courts - a role too public for the real backers to play - while the lists of attenders at county race balls always show many names associated with local trade and the professions. Even within the working class there was an increasing variety of attitudes towards play. It was not only that different sports had different appeals, with coopers, for example, said to be fond of cricket but not skittles, and the men of Wiltshire and Somerset devoted to stick fighting. But also the spread of Methodism created a new sub-section of workers prepared to reject all the old modes of play. There was, too, a gradual and still only partial softening and civilising that permeated further than strict religious revivalism, a process that made many less and less receptive to the delights of the bull-bait or the dog fight. There was no uninterrupted progress though. The rougher sports made a resurgence in London at least in the 1820s, with duck-shooting, badger-baiting, and rat-catching all in vogue. And while some places put an early stop to cock-fighting (Nottingham in 1804, for instance) other towns such as York were still building new pits in the early 1830s.

Moral pressures on popular recreation usually need allies other than the spiritual. Like all successful moral crusades - and this was certainly successful in part - they had to be in tune with the dominant class's other needs. Here, powerful backing came from those employers who had invested heavily in new plant and machinery and could not afford to see it lying idle. Race meetings looked all the more perfidious if they left the looms silent for two or three days.

Wakes that meant a late start to the working week and a semi-comatose work-force for the rest of it were indubitably sinful, and campaigns to abolish them never lacked funds or arguments. Long and regular working hours, far from being an untoward imposition, even took on the mantle of desirability, as beneficial to the workers' souls and salvation as they were to the employers' pockets. To ensure that the hours were worked, given the attractions of sport and play, it was morally right to keep wages as low as possible - 'the only way to make them temperate and industrious is to lay them under a necessity of labouring all the time they can spare from meals and sleep, in order to procure the common necessities of life.' Such claims came from all quarters. A Bingley surgeon told a parliamentary committee in 1818 that children did not need recreation at all, and a Scottish minister claimed that the factory was the best training ground for the 'volatile minds of youth.'

While the working classes themselves could hardly be expected to believe unreservedly in the moral claims of unremitting labour, their own movements and their spokesmen were equally reluctant to admit that recreation played any part in their programme for shorter hours. Typically, as in a pamphlet from the Pudsey reformers, they sought time 'for Fireside Improvement, Domestic Improvement, Literary Advancement by Evening Schools, and, above all, for Religious Instruction for all Factory Workers.' Play was low in the priorities of all the articulate classes.

It was the inarticulate, aided by minor scions of the very capitalist system which so hedged in popular recreation, who kept play alive, in spite of the dark days it had to endure. How popular sport adapted itself, and even flourished, in face of so much adversity, makes this one of the more remarkable of the many remarkable chapters in the history of the human urge to play, and to develop that play into ever new and challenging forms.

Play and the People
It is commonly accepted that the Industrial Revolution brought massive social change with it. It could hardly have been otherwise, given its dimensions. Coal production in England doubled between 1750 and 1800. Total industrial output probably did the same between 1780 and 1800. The distribution of the working population underwent correspondingly rapid change - by 1800 only some 35% of workers were directly engaged in agriculture, and this had dropped further to 16% by 1850. Villages like Bradford became towns, and towns became great cities. Leeds doubled to 123,000 in the first thirty years of the nineteenth century, and Sheffield grew from 45,000 to 91,000. Smaller centres like Blackburn, Bolton, and Oldham (a village of three or four hundred souls in the mid-eighteenth century) all doubled to around the 50,000 mark.

Popular recreation had to find ways of survival in alien conditions. It is little wonder that the great recorder of sporting habits, Joseph Strutt, writing in the middle of the period, should strike such predominantly pessimistic tones about contemporary play in his famous *Sports and Pastimes of the People of England*. He saw the old playing habits of his youth and of his forefathers fading, constricted on all sides, and for the most part he saw this accurately. What he did not appreciate were the new styles of recreation which were beginning to thrive, even in his own day.

The first pictures to come to mind are certainly those of old pursuits seeking to maintain themselves - even reassert themselves - against the conflicting backdrop of the town. What had been feasible in the countryside with a few hundred participants could become a virtual riot when it drew thousands into the streets. A bull-bait at Rochdale in 1820, at the end of the local fair, was typical of what could, and did, happen. The poor beast was staked on a six yard cord at the river's edge. It often retreated into three feet of water and many of the crowd followed, up to the knees. So great was the crush of spectators that a nearby bridge parapet collapsed, with nine deaths. While consciences were becoming more tender towards animal cruelty, it was the unruly behaviour of the mob rather than the pain to the bull that prompted press condemnation of the 'ignominious wickedness' of the event. Where there was a dearth of other sporting opportunities, the baiting of animals offered a considerable temptation. It needed no special arena and, as for the bulls, they were due for slaughter anyway, and there was the excuse that baiting was said to tenderise the meat. Nor was it just an occasional spectacle. In London, baiting had become regular and commercialised, happening in Black Boy Alley every night other than Saturday in 1805, with spectators charged 6d for admission. Dog-fighting was a customary Monday afternoon entertainment in Birmingham, among other places, and continued there surreptitiously well after the Cruelty to Animals Act of 1835. Rat-catching, too, became a flourishing city pursuit in the early decades of the nineteenth century when one of the age's unlikeliest sporting heroes was 'Billy the Dog', who achieved several years of fame for his speed in killing rodents. Wagered to kill 100 rats in ten minutes in November 1822, he did so

The Tom Cribb, near Haymarket

in 6 minutes 25 seconds, though there was suspicion that the rats were doped, and Billy even enjoyed posthumous fame, stuffed and mounted on the bar of the old boxing champion, Tom Cribb. Such was the commercialisation of this pursuit that one London publican claimed to have bought 26,000 live rats a year for the delectation of his customers and their dogs.

In a changed physical environment, even established sports such as cricket and horse-racing felt the pressure of rising and excitable populations, limited in their chances of letting off steam. Violence had always been likely to flare up in cricket matches, and its decline was only gradual. In 1776 disputing players in a game at Tilbury Fort had actually seized guns from the guardhouse and two deaths and other injuries resulted. Such incidents became less frequent, although a duel over a cricket dispute between two army officers in 1809 led to the death of one of them, and the game remained far from always gentile - not only were dogs on the field still likely to be shot (as they were on racecourses) but the players, even in the 1830s, had, according to the *Leicester Mercury* to be warned to 'keep back the convivial part' of the proceedings until after stumps were drawn, so that afternoon play did not show signs of 'weakness'!

As their numbers increased, racing crowds tended to become more rather than less boisterous, tempers heightened by the increasing amount of money involved, at all levels, in the sport. Any race that appeared to be fixed was the immediate occasion for rioting, while welshing on bets meant a horsewhipping and dumping into the nearest river. Even Ascot, for all its royal patronage, was better known in the 1830s for its tricksters and entertainers, its rigged gaming tables and its ladies dancing on stilts than it was for the quality of its racing. The number of races, though, rose steadily and the number of horses being raced rose from 600 to 1,000 between 1797 and 1822, and to 1,400 by the 1840s. There was no such increase in the honesty of the sport. In the 1844 Derby, at one of the turf's lowest ebbs, two four year-olds were smuggled into the race, one horse ran under a false name, the favourite lost its chance by foul riding, and another fancied horse was held back by its jockey, who had bet on another runner! With such machinations among the owners and riders, it was too much to expect race crowds to be models of restraint and sobriety.

A decline in sporting standards does not inevitably mean that a sport loses its popularity, especially in an age when there are few alternatives. The prize-ring, for instance, by no means went out of existence when it lost most of its upper-class support in the mid-1820s. The number of fights, if not their individual significance, grew steadily, and the columns of challenges in *Bell's Life in London* grew longer and longer until well into the second half of the century. Prize-fighting might fall into the hands of publicans, money-lenders, and small-time financial adventurers, but it catered for the crowds and so far as the forces of law and order were concerned these crowds were usually well-behaved - it seldom took more than a magistrate and a constable or two to move them along to another site. It was around the fight itself that the irregularities grew, especially in the second quarter of the century. Fights were fixed, refereeing became less reliable, and crowds invaded the ring more and more often, intimidating boxers and officials alike. By the 1850s the darker shades of support for the ring had come to dominate, and the sport sank gradually further and further into the lower reaches of urban sub-culture.

The changes taking place within the working classes themselves did not for the time being, favour the emergence of national sports and games. The systematisation of, for instance, horse-racing and cricket, continued to be promoted largely from above. Popular recreation was diverse, both in its styles and in the opportunities for its enjoyment. If the country was changing rapidly, it was also changing unevenly. Long-established towns which grew gradually, such as Exeter, Bristol, and Norwich, suffered much less upheaval than new settlements which suddenly transformed villages into near-cities. Even in cities, the working population's experience could differ widely from place to place. Birmingham, with its small-scale workshop production, remained outside the factory system until the 1860s, some hundred years after it had been established in such places as lowland Scotland, Lancashire, and parts of the Midlands. It was not only city life which provided few recreational outlets - Gloucestershire villagers were described in 1803 as spending their one day of rest 'some in ale-houses, others at pitch-and-toss, fives, and other games.' Popular play had to be opportunistic, to take advantage of the time and the place as they presented themselves - or could be seized upon.

As to leisure time, the factory system made little provision for it. Twelve or more hours a day, six days a week was the rule. Where textile mills retained the old practice of stopping work earlier on Saturday than on other days, it was unusual for this to be much before 6.00 pm, and if there were agreed breaks for fairs or wakes, overtime was commonly worked to make up for them. None the less, in spite of the apparent strictness of the regimes, there were many sporting events held in the mill towns, particularly pedestrian contests and prize-fights, and the number of race meetings in the industrial areas increased steadily. It is clear from the employers' protests that these could half empty the factory from time to time, and that it was only when there was a surfeit of labour that they could impose the strict discipline they sought. In domestic, small-scale manufacturing the opportunities for regular leisure were much greater, but at a price. Work-shops were frequently silent on Mondays, often remained so on Tuesday, but at the expense of frantic working, sixteen hours a day or more, for the remaining days of the week. It made Monday the great sporting day of the first half of the nineteenth century, with Tuesday (much the favourite prize-fight day) a close second. In Birmingham, for instance, the local journal commented in 1840 that Monday was 'generally kept as a holiday by a great proportion of the working classes,' and described the local recreations as ranging from marbles to dog-fighting, and from bar-games to cricket, though the most commonly enjoyed pastime seems to have been drinking.

The working population and their immediate allies were finding their own solutions, however limited they might be, to the recreational problems of the Industrial Revolution. The most consistent of these allies was, as always, the publican. With the loss of playing space, especially in towns, and more efficient policing driving play from the streets, the publican's facilities became all the more important. Many still had their fields attached and some of these had been enclosed for a specific sporting purpose, notably Lords and Trent Bridge. Others were used as running grounds for pedestrian contests, and still more as all-purpose recreation areas for the clientele. Rising urban property values, though, were gradually taking their toll at the beginning of the Victorian years and in Birmingham, for example, the Bowling Green Tavern, Holloway Head, was being described in a notice for sale in 1848 as having the only bowling green left

Behind the Fleur-de-Lis, Stoke-sub-Hamden, Somerset stands this imposing fives wall

in the centre of the city. As well as providing for every sort of sport from quoits to pigeon-racing, acting as a betting shop, and the local headquarters of activities such as prize-fighting, some publicans went to great lengths in producing new facilities, among the most conspicuous from this period being the fives walls, still visible in some half dozen south Somerset villages, massive structures designed to bring fives players away from the church towers (where they were distinctly and increasingly unwelcome) and nearer to the bar and the beer pump. In the 1840s they were attracting hundreds of spectators.

The contribution of the publican to recreation during the later eighteenth and earlier nineteenth centuries is hard to overstate. It covered not only the rowdier sports and games associated with drinking, but extended into the broader field of entertainment - dramatics, music, flower shows, race dinners, and many such other functions relied on the innkeeper. His tavern, too, was the obvious meeting place for sporting clubs, and the location from which the local races were administered. It was fitting that, eventually, a new age of sport should be ushered in by a meeting at a hostelry, at the Freemason's Tavern in London's Great Queen Street, in October 1863. This was to lead to the foundation of the Football Association. It set the seal on the public house's role in fostering the transition from the old sporting world to one that would be regularised, approved, and orderly. But that lay in the future. In the early part of the nineteenth century there was still much gloom to be lifted. The difficulty was that, while the people sought out whatever ways to play and entertainment they could contrive, the middle and upper-classes would only look on with a mixture of puzzlement and distaste. They found popular leisure presented a problem, and began to search for the means of its solution.

The 'Problem' of Leisure

Traditionalists and radicals alike were concerned over the recreational choices which seemed to confront the working man - only occasionally did they extend the concern to include his womenfolk. The worker would apparently have no sanctioned leisure time at all, or would take what he could in anarchic and uncontrollable fashions. The critics discovered what the labourer already knew - that the innkeeper was indeed the prime provider for his recreation - and the awareness was not encouraging. One of the clearest expressions of the current concerns came from Lord John Manners, ally of the young Disraeli, who noted the frequent contemporary references to the growing and widespread lack of spirit in the people, once noted 'for their love of manly sports and their sturdy good humour.' He put down their growing 'habits and thoughts of discontent and moroseness' to the 'loss of those wholesome recreations' which were formerly common.

If the difficulties were widely acknowledged, the cures were hard to find. Manners, writing in the 1840s, wanted a revival of the former holy days and of the sports that went with them, developing a frequent theme of the past few decades. Twenty years earlier, a writer in the *Sporting Magazine* had urged that the lower orders should be allowed 'to lay aside their implements of labour, and for a short time enjoy those festivities which their inclinations may lead them to prefer.' They were policies which might have had some success in Sussex or Kentish villages, but hardly made much appeal to employers in Bolton or Blackburn. The other intended direction of reform was to remould the 'inclinations' of the working classes, to turn them away from the obsolescent sports of the past, and to point them towards more wholesome play. 'Rational Recreation,' as it became known, was never very clearly defined, but tended towards sedate walks, country dancing, gymnastic exercises, and regulated 'rural sports'. Some noted the persistent tendency for change to bear most heavily on the working classes, as Sydney Smith remarked over the restrictions on Sunday play, while other correspondents to the sporting press questioned how sporting gentlemen could themselves oppose the already limited recreations of the masses. Occasionally, though, there is evidence of middle-class dissatisfaction as well. 'Old Wykehamist' was complaining in *The Times* in 1843 that London offered few facilities - paddle steamers had made rowing on the Thames hazardous, there was only one rackets court and that at a public house, while quoits 'have fled for refuge and encouragement to the suburban pothouse.'

The general feeling of the time is clear. Recreation was in slump, and it was showing in the national character. Testing out this thesis was one of the minor factors in the launch of the Crimean War a decade later.

Private and public efforts had been made to remedy the ills from the turn of the century. The best known is that of Robert Owen, whose factory improvements included the hiring of a band and dancing masters for the exercise of his work-force. Whether there is much truth in a rival's claim that the dancing and drills tired the workers out and drove them across to his factory, the general reception of such efforts at recreational betterment was at best lukewarm. Gifts of playing spaces might have more effect, at least in the immediate locality, so long as their use was not too patronisingly controlled. The Earl of Dartmouth set aside four acres in West Bromwich, for instance, and former MP for Reading set aside a field near his Berkshire house 'as a play-ground for the children, or whoever likes to play.' Such gestures were likely to bring more widespread satisfaction than the earlier ambitious substitution of a performance of Handel's *Messiah* instead of the customary Easter bull-bait at Engton in Staffordshire!

Attempts to provide local sports were quite widespread, and also diverse in their styles. Rural revels could cover a whole range of possibilities from corrupt versions of old country play - grinning through horse collars, eating treacle with a fork, chasing a greased pig, and the like - to conscious attempts to promote sports that had some athletic integrity. There were, for example, Colonel Mason's festival of rural sports at Necton, Norfolk, first held in 1817, and the Till-side Border Games, established by Robert Paxton in 1836, 'for the encouragement of athletic exercises on the English and Scottish Borders,' and characterised by track and field events which looked much more strongly towards the organised future of athletics than to the miscellany of often esoteric contests of much pedestrianism. Its one frivolity, a sack race, was described as 'trivial of itself,' but affording great diversion! They were to be followed later in the century by the Much Wenlock Olympics and, tapping revived Scottish nationalism, a succession of Highland Games.

Interesting as such innovations were, their impact on the mass of the population was slim. Even locally, they were often restricted to the deserving - like Sunday School outings, they were rewards for good attendance and modest deportment, and were doubtless equally cyclical in any effects they had! Less formally provided revelling could sometimes seem designed to exploit the needs and ignorance of the poor for the amusement of the rich, who would throw heated coins down from inn balconies to enjoy the scramble for them, or give prizes for the ugliest grimace. The workers themselves sometimes reacted. At Huddersfield they held a meeting and resolved not to take part in the celebration of Sir J.W. Ramsden's coming of age in 1852, finding the proposed 'sports' highly objectionable and urging their fellows, 'out of self-respect', and 'regard for moral well-being' not to participate.

The leisure ambitions of the articulate sections of the working classes tended, where they existed at all, towards rational recreation rather than these 'new contrived sports of sack-racing, grinning, etc'. Their support went in the direction of reading rooms and debating halls, and when the more skilled workers became involved in the Mechanics Institutes, these seldom made any provision for sports. A gymnasium provided at the Manchester Institute gave way to a new library, and was not replaced, while only a few Yorkshire Institutes managed to secure their own cricket grounds. In any event, the Institutes were gradually appropriated by the middle class, in their own search for outside refreshment as the century drew on.

Apart from these various local attempts to make some provision for the recreation of the workers and their families, there were also national initiatives which, directly or indirectly, had some impact on the situation. These stemmed from a growing dislike of cruelty to men and animals (but not necessarily in that order), from a preoccupation with the need to preserve open spaces, with public hygiene, and with working conditions, especially those of women and children. Some measures were suppressive, like that against cruel sports, which met with considerable scattered resistance - the inspectors brought at least 13 prosecutions for cock-fighting between 1838 and 1841. The Factory Acts began their gradual (and at first uncertain) amelioration of the worst industrial working conditions, and members of parliament began to show concern for public health. There was a campaign for the provision of public parks, the General Enclosure Act of 1845 made it more difficult to deprive cities of all their open spaces, and a year later local councils, in the interests of hygiene, were allowed to provide public baths. Already Liverpool had taken its own initiative, and many towns and cities soon followed, but if the intentions behind the baths centred on cleanliness, it was soon their swimming facilities which became their main attraction.

So it was with much public provision for the people's leisure. Their recreational wants seldom coincided with what was thought proper for their enjoyment. Public parks were needed most of all for playing in, and only in part for sedate walks and band concerts, though the suspension of the latter on Sunday afternoons in London was enough to provoke rioting in 1855. It meant that late-comers like Birmingham had the advantage over innovators such as Liverpool, able to provide for football and cricket pitches, as well as for ornament and decorum.

This was where the answer to the 'problem' of leisure was to lie - not in some newly contrived recreational activity prescribed from above, but in the games and sports that were already there, that were intrinsic to the people's own sporting experience. It was the refining of the old sports to bring them nearer to the expectations of the new moral and social order that produced the answer, particularly with the later addition to their ranks of that perennial game of the people, football, itself to be uniquely transformed into the winter pastime of the coming age.

All the existing sports made some attempt, greater or less, to renew, revise, and regulate themselves, to make themselves less offensive to changing tastes. The task, and the efforts at betterment, varied considerably from sport to sport. Cricket was the most successful, starting as it did from the most favoured base, as 'the good old English game.' While its reputation was less chequered than that of rival pursuits, the early nineteenth-century game still had its gambling, its stakes, the hard drinking of players and spectators, and the rowdiness at and after matches. Gambling regulations remained in the laws of the game until the 1880s, and betting was still significant until at least mid-century. But efforts at improvement were being made, and gradually had their effect. Gambling was banned from Lords in the 1820s, though it took some time to disappear completely, and at least one player was banned for allegedly throwing a match. The play was speeded up and better regulated, and fixtures began to take on some recognisable annual sequence. Crowds grew in numbers without growing in disorder and by the late 1840s the country was ready for the spectacle of William Clarke's 'All England XI' touring and taking the game to all parts, enjoying the new-found freedom brought by the railway.

Racing had a much harder furrow to plough to achieve wholesale acceptance, and it is arguable that only its strong aristocratic connections kept it alive through the middle decades of the century. Race meetings aroused strong and contradictory feelings. They were either celebrated as great occasions for communal enjoyment that defied class barriers (which was only marginally true, given the segregation of the spectators) or were roundly condemned for their violence and gambling, their actual danger, and the magnet they presented to tricksters and whores. The Jockey Club did what it could. Its members now had more frequent interests in racing away from Newmarket, especially as other meetings increased their prize money and their status, and the Club, if half reluctantly, began to extend its authority more widely over the sport. At the start of the century it began to publicise its rules more fully, and then took the important step of only agreeing to adjudicate on cases arising from meetings where its own rules were followed. It was an effective means of distancing and weakening the less reputable events. It was, though, to take years of vigorous reforming leadership, first from Lord George Bentinck, and then Admiral Rous to bring racing some tenuous respectability, a respectability which was then secured by the powerful support of the Prince of Wales, the future Edward VII.

Cricket and horse-racing would succeed in their reformations. They would pass into a fully modern sporting world without fundamental change to their nature as sports or to their basic ethos and organisation. It was to be otherwise with those other two sporting attractions inherited from the past, pedestrianism and pugilism. Pedestrianism seemed at first to be set fair for growth. It was the first spectator sport to identify and exploit the rising market for commercially based play in the industrial areas, and the first to spot the new opportunity that early closing was giving for Saturday afternoon events. Its promoters were beginning to move the emphasis of their events from Mondays to Saturdays as early as the 1840s. This keen eye for profit, though, had also within it the key to the sport's collapse. Too many of the organisers and performers set financial gain above sporting integrity. Two-man contests depending on speed and strength were much easier to manipulate than horse-racing or cricket matches, and fixed matches became as much the rule as the exception. Pedestrianism had always had an existence which, however much it had enjoyed upper-class support, had never depended on it. As that support disappeared, from a combination of distrust and changed tastes, commercial pedestrianism fell further and further into disrepute. It could only diminish, go on its own narrowing way as a professional entertainment, and be replaced in the second half of the century by its new and aggressively amateur form - modern athletics.

A similar fate was almost inevitable for pugilism, with its additional handicap of illegality. After the decline of its honesty and order with the withdrawal of aristocratic support in the 1820s, there were several attempts at resuscitation, but all were short-lived. The Fair Play Club in the late 1820s was immediately undermined by a patently thrown major fight, while some thirty years later there was the Pugilists' Benevolent Association, a strange mixture of friendly society, trades union, and sport governing body - and soon ineffective in any of the roles. Changing inclinations among the spectators, more efficient policing from the authorities, and the attraction of North America to the pugilists, all contributed to the sport's demise. Again a new amateur form had to appear, under the Marquess of Queensberry's Rules, before the ring could edge again into sporting acceptance.

The first lights of sport's new dawn began to glimmer from a quite unexpected quarter. It came from the two ancient universities and their decision to challenge each other to a rowing race on the River Thames. For some years the event caused little stir, until interest began to be aroused, and the crowds flocked annually to the banks of the river. What drew them there was competition in a new mode, between potentially equal sides, unsullied by stake money or other financial considerations, with the prospect of totally honest and fair competition without any hint of pre-arranged spectacle. These were to be the characteristics of sport in the new style. Here lay the real answer to the 'problem' of leisure, even though few if any could see it as such at the time.

The Provincialisation of Sport
Another element in the reshaping of sport in the first half of the nineteenth century was geographical. The past dominance of London and south-eastern England became diluted - in some sports it was decisively displaced - and the whole emphasis began to shift to the regions and to other parts of the kingdom.

The best and more readily plotted example of dissemination is provided by cricket, which did not fully emerge from its south-eastern heartland until after the Napoleonic Wars, spreading like the ripples on a pool, becoming country-wide when the railway took the touring professionals to all parts of the island. Along with this widespread diffusion went the loss of unquestioned dominance which south-eastern players had previously enjoyed. In the second quarter of the century the axis of the game was moving into the North and Midlands, with cities such as Nottingham and Sheffield becoming as important centres as London. Even more notable was the way in which pedestrian contests followed the movements in population. From being a scattered sport loosely weighted towards the south-east, it became preponderantly based on the new industrial areas. As early as 1838, of the many events reported in *Bell's Life in London* for the first six months of the year, only a handful took place south of the Trent, with common venues in Manchester, Doncaster, and Oldham.

At the other extreme, of course, were sporting activities which had always resisted the metropolitan magnet, and remained nationally or regionally rooted. Pre-eminently there was golf in Scotland, where there was curling, 'a manly and difficult game' according to one commentator in 1837, played by all classes, with clubs 'where a small subscription affords the curlers' standing dish, beef and greens.' The Welsh had their bandy and the Irish their shinty, both versions of the stick and ball game, while in the English regions there was wrestling in the celtic fringes, singlestick, cudgelling and fives in Wessex, and ice-skating in the Fen country.

Horse-racing and prize-fighting, the two sports which ran universally through the islands, both demonstrated a notable degree of provincialisation. In England, Newmarket began to be left behind from the 1820s onwards by courses such as Doncaster and York which offered higher prize money, while the sport continued to flourish over the rest of the islands. In Ireland, there were 15 to 20 meetings annually, apart from the full-week races four times a year at the Curragh. Courses ranged from Enniskillen in Fermanagh to Rathkeale in Limerick and Mallow in County Cork, and Irish racing saw itself as very much part of the British scene, referring its disputes to the Jockey Club at Newmarket. In Scotland, the sport had a history stretching back at least as far as its counterpart south of the border, and at the turn of the century racing was both widespread dated with a mile or two mile race level. Griffith will be at Mr Low's, Green Dragon, Fleet-street, on Tuesday evening next, prepared to make a match.

JOHN SYDDALL of Radcliffe will run any of the following half a mile, and give 10 yards start, for £25 a side, viz, Simon Clarkson, Joseph Pinder, John Sewell or John Tetlow (both of Oldham), or John Howard of Bradford, or the celebrated John Howard 700 yards, at Bellevue, Manchester. By sending £5 to Mr J. Holden, White Lion, Long Millgate, Manchester, and articles to him at old Jerry Jem's, Preston, a match can be made.

YOUNG ANNAL of Pottery Field hearing that John Brown of Hunslet is not satisfied with his late defeat, will run him again on the same terms, for £5 a side; or William Carter of Newton 130 yards; or take two yards start of Tip Ripley, or Johnson (both of Newton) in 120 yards, for £5 or £10 a side. A match can be made at the Boiler Makers' Arms, Pottery Field, Hunslet, Leeds.

HARRY WATSON of Bradford will run any of the following one mile, for £25 a side, viz, Ely Parkin of Huddersfield, Rant of Holmfirth, Cob Heaton of Netherton, Bincliffe of Raistrick, Jonathan Bincliffe of Raistrick, or give Pummell of Manningham 15 yards, or Gallick of Horton 30 yards in a mile. Matches can be made by sending £5 to us, and articles to the Beckett's Arms, Bradford.

T. WOOD (the Worksop Novice) will accept the challenge of Isaac Howarth of Sheffield to run 200 yards, or run Barlow of Stockport, Norris of Nottingham, Samuel Williamson of Levenshulme 200 yards, at Worksop, on a fair turnpike road, or take £3 to run at Bellevue, Manchester, on the 23d Feb, for £25 or £50 a side. His money is ready at Eyre's, Cheshire Cheese, Watson-street, Manchester.

THOMAS CARNEY of Manchester thinks Sully of Arnold is bouncing; but if he means running he will meet him half way between home and home, or allow him reasonable expenses to run 140 yards, at Bellevue, in a month or five weeks from the first deposit, for £20 or £25 a side; or J. Edmondson of Wakefield on the same terms. A letter addressed to Mr J. Holden, White Lion, Long Milgate, Manchester, will be attended to.

JAMES MALPAS will run John Smith of Stockport 140 yards, for £10 or £20 a side; or Thomas Barlow of the same place 200 yards, for £10 or £25 a side, in a month from the first deposit. He will be at the White Lion, Long Milgate, Manchester, on Monday next, from seven to ten o'clock, prepared to make a match.

JOSEPH HINCHLIFFE (alias Runt) of Holmforth will run Phillip Shaw of White Abbey one mile over Bellevue Course, for £20 or £25 a side; Jonathan Bintley of Rustrick one mile, or Thomas Bintley two miles for the like sum. The money will be ready at Mitchell's, Moss Tavern, Holmfirth, any night next week.

G. SHAW will run Frederick Broome of the Haymarket 120 yards, for £5 a side, on the Copenhagen Grounds, in three weeks from the first deposit, and meet him at the Royal Pair, Gloster-grove East, Old Brompton, on Monday night, to make the match; if not accepted, he will run H. Rubridge if he will give three yards start in 100, for the like amount.

JOHN SNAREY of Witton Park is now ready to accept the challenge of Thomas Hutchinson of Gateshead to run one mile on Gilliate Moor, Durham, for £15 a side, in six weeks from the first deposit. If articles are sent to Mr J. Booth's, Railway Bridge Inn, Etherley, near Bishop Auckland, and £5 to us, a match can be made.

THOMAS LYON (late of Bolton, but now of Leeds) will run Frank Crossley (late of Bury, but now in Leeds) 200 yards, and give him two yards start, for from £10 to £25 a side. The match can be made at the Boiler Makers' Arms, Pottery Field, Hunslet, near Leeds; or John Hinds of Leeds can be accommodated on the same terms.

THOMAS FENWICK of Lanchester will run Wm. Hind of Carlisle 200 yards,

Bell's Life in London (25 January 1852)

and generous in its prize money. Edinburgh might not dominate the sport to the same extent as the Curragh did in Dublin, but its six-day meetings would boast a King's Plate, while Ayr, at the same period in the early nineteenth century, would include a 100 guinea gold cup among its prizes for a three-day meeting, which included matches as well as races. Lamberton was another course offering a gold cup, while the Caledonian, Dumfries and Galloway meeting in 1810 stretched over a full week and included two 100-guinea races. Some Scottish races were certainly less successful. At Kelso in 1806, for example, the second day was without a race at all, perhaps a reason for the mounting of additional attractions in later years - in 1822, these included 100 wrestlers in a competition and a blind pedestrian.

The more distant meetings were not slow in taking up new racing fashions. Both Scotland and Wales were to the fore in mounting steeplechases in the early 1820s, when the sport was very much in its infancy. In Wales, racing was the one spectator sport to have developed to any appreciable extent. In 1806, for instance, there were some half-dozen meetings, with Swansea's three-day event including two highly staked matches, one for £200 and one for £100.

The geographical changes affecting the turf, which had long been a nation-wide sport, were matters of emphasis, raising the status of racing in the provinces. The changes in the geographical shape of pugilism were more wholesale. Until the 1820s, the sport's unchallenged centre was London, and any fighter, whether from Bristol, Dublin, or wherever, had to go to London for the big match-making and the national fame. As the upper class patronage of the ring fell away, London ceased to have the monopoly of such financial support as remained. The money, and the crowds, were as likely to be in the Midlands and the North, and the policing there often not as strict as in the Home Counties. For some years in the 1830s, when its own Jem Ward was champion, Liverpool had the reputation of being the 'metropolis of milling' - it was the decade, incidentally, which also brought both the railway and the first Grand National to the city. Then, in turn, the Midlands provided a string of champions, and while the London ring continued to sponsor some important fights, it existed now on a more equal parity with the regional circuits. One reason for the brief revival of prize-fighting's national interest in the late 1850s was, in fact, the emergence at last of a bright and skilful London fighter, in Tom Sayers.

All the home countries played their parts in the history of British pugilism, and none more than the Irish. From Michael Ryan's two hard fights with the champion, Tom Johnson, in the late 1780s to John Langan's brave contests with Tom Spring in the 1820s, the Irish produced a host of good performers, and some not quite so good. All of them, though, could be assured of glowing reports from Pierce Egan, the virtual founder of the sporting press, proud of his own Hibernian ancestry, and always prepared to lavish his imaginative and ornate prose upon their efforts. While fighting in Ireland itself was popular and widespread, the big purses were in England. Irish fights tended to be unregulated, disorderly, and seldom for more than £50 a side. Typically, when John Langan beat Carney for the Irish championship, before coming across to challenge in England, a riot swamped the end of the contest.

The Irish enthusiasm for prize-fighting made it a favourite touring ground for boxers giving sparring exhibitions, a common way for well-known pugilists to profit from their fame. Some settled there, and in the 1820s Dublin became a hive of boxing enterprise. Tom Gregson, who had fought bravely against

John Gully for the championship, founded a school for self-defence - in what had previously been the Royal Academy! Later he joined a whole band of ex-pugilists to run Dublin taverns. His was in Moor Street, his fellow Englishman, Jack Carter, was in Barrack Street, and, briefly, Ireland's own flamboyant Dan Donnelly had an inn in Pill Lane. Later, Tom Reynolds, the most articulate of fighters who wrote a *Defence of Pugilism*, and had introduced his fellow countrymen, Langan and Byrne, to the English ring, ran his public house in Abbey Street 'with great regularity' until his death.

Where the turf and the ring flourished, so usually did the cock-pit. Ireland was no exception, and was soon following the English example of making matches described as being between counties - such as that between the Gentlemen of Armagh and those of King's County over five days for 1,000 guineas in Dublin in 1808. As usual with such events, heavy betting was reported. Wales, by contrast, had little reputation for producing prize-fighters or mounting fights. A few Welsh fighters, such as Ned Turner, made their mark in the London ring, and there was obviously support for fights, at least near the borders with England, but few are reported. When James was defeated by Penk in Flintshire in 1822, large crowds gathered and all the beds in the town were taken. This, though, was a rare event. Hickman's fight with Robinson in 1827, for instance, with £200 at stake, only took place in Monmouthshire because the Hereford magistrates had forced them over the border. At the same time, the Welsh did have their own popular sports, such as bandy, which, like the Irish hurling, was an embryonic form of hockey. It was said in 1830 to be particularly favoured in the Vale of Glamorgan, and often played on the sands. There would be twenty or thirty players a side, wearing distinguishing team favours on their left arms, and they would start in a line facing each other. It was obviously a game which had achieved some degree of organisation and sophistication.

The Scots produced fewer prizefighters than the Irish, but did have the distinction of nurturing William Fuller, who was eventually to introduce the British style of boxing to the United States through his New York gymnasium, this after a remarkable international sporting career during which he had also been clerk of the course at Valenciennes in France! Another Scot to achieve fighting fame, though with a sadder end, was Sandy M'Kay, a giant of a man, who was so badly mauled in a fight with the Irishman, Simon Byrne, than he died within twenty-four hours. There was another, and more famous Scottish sportsman associated with this particular fight, namely Captain Allardyce Barclay, who took charge of the final stages of M'Kay's training. Barclay, a wealthy landowner, had a long and varied athletic career, culminating in what became the classic pedestrian event, the 'Barclay Match' of covering 1,000 miles in 1,000 hours, which he achieved on Newmarket Heath in July, 1808. Subsequently he trained Tom Cribb for his second encounter with the black challenger Tom Molyneux, who had come near to beating him in the first bout. His regime in the Highlands brought down Cribb's weight, improved his wind and strength, and led to a comparatively easy victory.

This was not the only link between the prize-ring and athletics in Scotland, where pedestrianism was as popular as in England. After the Yorkshireman, Robinson, had fought and beaten the Glaswegian Crosbie near Edinburgh in 1825, he went on to defeat a Glasgow pedestrian in a 400 yards race less than an hour later! Within a few years the Six Feet Club in

Edinburgh was holding athletics meetings which had a distinct air of modernity, including as they did a steeplechase, 'hop, step and leap,' putting the shot, and throwing the hammer. The spectators we are told, included many ladies. Already, too, Highland Games were coming into vogue. The Northern Games at Inverness in 1821 had featured 'tossing the cabber-tree,' 'throwing the sledge hammer,' and 'leaping the plaid,' as well as foot races.

There was, of course, one sport largely confined to Scotland that was eventually to assume world-wide significance. Golf had had a limited existence in England since James I's courtiers had introduced it, but it still remained firmly rooted in its native land, so far as any extensive following was concerned. Golf in England seems to have been confined, in any organised fashion, to the Blackheath Club, whose doings did reach the press. Most of its players were apparently emigré Scots, such as William Innes, from Linlithgow, 'father of the Blackheath Golf Club' according to his obituary. It was Scots, too, who were largely responsible for the first spread of the sport in England with the founding of the Old Manchester Club in 1818.

In Scotland itself, golf stood out above the decline that marked many sporting activities in the eighteenth century. Societies and clubs were formed in many places, usually with membership drawn from the leisured and profes-sional classes, although the Edinburgh Burgess Society, founded in 1773, was broader based, including, according to the sport's historian, 'bakers, gold-smiths, glaziers, grocers, hairdressers, masons and ropemakers.' Uniforms identified club members, as they did in other sports of the day, that of St Andrews consisting of a red jacket with yellow buttons and a 'frock' of buff with a red cap. It was St Andrews, too, which received the crown's stamp of approval when William IV became its patron and authorised the title of 'Royal and Ancient.'

Bowling, too, survived more systematically in Scotland than in England, where urbanisation increasingly caused greens to be given over for building. Every Scottish town was said still to have its green and the game flourished there so thoroughly that it provided the eventual basis for the future organisation of the sport, a process set decisively under way when 200 members of Scottish bowling clubs met in Glasgow Town Hall in 1848, in order to outline the first formal regulations for the game.

That it was in Scotland that bowling and golf pioneered their organisational structures was indicative of the geographical change which was taking the monopoly of sporting leadership away from London and the south-eastern corner of England. It was a tendency that would continue during the rest of the century, no more emphatically than in the future national game, which would see the whole original membership of the English Football League coming from the North and the Midlands, and new southern clubs looking largely to imported Scots to get their game off the ground at all.

The Living Past IV

Great houses, inns, Mechanics' Institutes, parks and swimming baths, and old sporting venues may all carry memories of this age of the Industrial Revolution.

The contemporary prosperity of the upper classes and their readiness to invest heavily in their increasingly exclusive sporting pursuits is reflected in many country houses. They often had extensive hunting and racing establish-

The Duke of Bedford's stables with the new tennis court and riding house at Woburn Abbey

Worcester Racecourse, the site of the Spring v Langham championship fight in 1824

ments, usually very well accommodated - where the houses are now open to the public, these facilities are favourite locations for shops and tea-rooms! Given the class bias of the press and its readership, hunts were often described in considerable geographical detail, and there is extensive literature on the sport.

Geographical precision over pugilistic sites, on the other hand, is usually much more difficult. It was a fugitive sport and its sites were often the result of one-off opportunism, leaving no marks on the landscape. The exceptions are the handful of important fights (and the numerous minor ones, for hurriedly collected purses) which took place on racecourses. Epsom, Brighton, Ludlow, Warwick and, most notably, Worcester, where Spring fought Langham for the championship in 1824, all provided relatively safe venues, but usually only briefly. More sustained locations were Molesey Hurst and Bushey Park, in south-west London, and under the protection of the future William IV during the Regency, Coleshill Castle, near Birmingham, in the 1840s, and at a humbler level still, the Dartford Marshes somewhat later.

As with most sports, the administration of pugilism depended upon the public house. Its 'headquarters' was, for many years, The Castle, Holborn, and subsequently at Jem Burn's Rising Sun, Alex Keene's Three Tuns in Soho, and Alex Reid's Lowndes Arms. Inns, however, while many do have historical sporting significance, are often not as fruitful sources as they promise to be. Of over fifty of them with prize-fighting associations in London, only one is identifiable from its original name - the Lowndes Arms, unexpectedly sited off the King's Road, in Belgravia, and built originally for the construction workers when the district was being developed in the 1820s. Other original buildings doubtless still exist, but under altered names. By contrast, sporting names, sometimes implying antiquity, are often spuriously attached to licensed premises old and new. London aside, it is clear from the sporting press that virtually every

Victorian town had its sporting public house where matches were made, stakes handed over, and the winnings presented.

The first enclosed sporting arenas on any scale appeared from about the 1820s for pedestrian events. Some were doubtless rudimentary (there are sometimes complaints about the tightness of the track) but they were certainly soon widespread. Among many others were Green Lanes, Tottenham; Copenhagen House, Islington (the 'Old Cope' of diverse sporting fame); Rosemary Racing Grounds, Commercial Road, Peckham; Hounslow Enclosure Ground; Vauxhall Gardens, at both Birmingham and Manchester; Hyde Park Ground, Sheffield; Birchfield, Birmingham; Three Mile Oak, Birmingham; Ash Inn, Heaton Norris, near Stockport; Snipe Inn, Ashton under Lyne, and the White Mare Pool, Newcastle.

There was also increasing sporting activity over the rest of the British Isles, reflected, for instance, in the number of race meetings. In Scotland, they included Ayr, Bogside, Dumfries, Edinburgh (Leith Sands, in earlier years), Hamilton, Fife Hunt, Kelso, Lamberton, Paisley, Perth, and Stirling. Irish meetings included Ballinrode, Callan, the Curragh, Birr, Cloghan, Down, Enniskillen, Lanesborough, Limerick, Loughrea, Mallow, Maidenhill, Maze, Rathkeal, Tuam, Tullow, and Gort, while Wales had Abergavenny, Aberystwyth, Brecon, Cardiff, Holywell, Haverfordwest, Knighton, Monmouth, Swansea, Tremadoc, and Wrexham.

The Lowndes Arms retains both its original name and appearance

Specific instances of flourishing local sport are already known, and more are likely to be revealed, even from quite early in the nineteenth century. Norwich, for example, which became an important sporting centre in the ten years after Waterloo, soon boasted its own Pugilistic Club, and mounted three or four major fights, one of them attracting 1,000 carriages, packed with ladies as well as gentlemen. Regional and local sports also flourished - knurr and spell in the North, fives and singlestick fighting in the West Country, and there is more to be found out both about these and others. There is much scope virtually everywhere for local enquiry into parks and recreational grounds, swimming baths, Mechanics' Institutes, and other early Victorian institutions with possible sporting relevance.

From the beginning of the nineteenth century contemporary written evidence, whether by way of the press or in documentary records, becomes too extensive to attempt to list. Local record offices and reference libraries are the starting point. The best secondary source for the immediate background is Hugh Cunningham, *Leisure in the Industrial Revolution* (London, 1980). More specific to sport, Richard Holt's *Sport and the British: A Modern History* (Oxford, 1990) comes into the picture, strengthening as it proceeds towards the mid-Victorian age, while Dennis Brailsford, *Sport, Time, and Society* (London and New York, 1991) expands some of the themes touched on in this chapter. Among useful works on individual sports are Geoffrey Cousins, *Golf in Britain: A Social History from the Beginnings to the Present Day* (London, 1975), and Hylton Cleaver, *A History of Rowing* (London, 1957). Much the most authoritative work on racing is Wray Vamplew, *The Turf: A Social and Economic History of Horse Racing* (London, 1976), though there is interesting descriptive material in, for instance, Dorothy Laird, *Royal Ascot* (London, 1976) and Michael Ayres and Gary Newbon, *Over the Sticks: The Sport of National Hunt Racing* (Newton Abbot, 1971). For a geographical view of sport, there is J.R. Bale, *Sport and Place: A Geography of Sport in England, Scotland and Wales* (London, 1982).

5

Playing Fair

The great recreational discovery of the later Victorians was that sport could be equated with virtue. It was no easy route to this new revelation. There were many contributing and converging pathways, and the new vision of play had not only to be shorn of the sins of the past, it had also to acquire positive moral qualities. It had to embrace equal competition between equal numbers to well-known published rules, and these rules had to be justly upheld. It had to be pursued for its own sake, without any pecuniary consideration, but not for mere pleasure alone - part of the vision was that games, whether honestly won or honestly lost, promoted individual strength of character and so served the national need. While the rarefied qualities which the new play demanded could hardly be expected to pervade the whole population - they were too exacting - there seemed every prospect that the masses themselves would have some share in the benefits brought by the fulfilment of the athletic ideal.

The Victorian era was the great age of the middle classes. As its members grew more assured of their rising dominance, they felt more able to allow themselves some further ration of leisure and recreation. They would only desert their old suspicions of play, however, if play itself could bring itself into harmony with their own values and concepts of decency. New expectations, which gradually permeated downwards through the social scale, brought new responses within sports and games. These were aided by a host of new technologies, which made travel and communication easier and which, applied to the actual practices of games, made steadily for greater subtlety and skill. Moreover, the rediscovery of the desirability of leisure, and an overall level of prosperity, made the granting of official free time a possibility. Saturday afternoon emerged as the great playing occasion, and a range of games appeared which admirably suited its enjoyment.

It was all too great a change to be left to accidents of mere chance. It had its agencies for promotion in the public schools, and for its organisation and regulation in the new national sporting bodies. A reign that began with vigorous attempts to put down cock-fighting and bring prize-fights to an end concluded with test matches against Australia and crowds of 75,000 at Crystal Palace for the FA Cup Final.

Sport, Science, and Technology

Technological progress has constantly tended to make sport more skilful, more exciting, and with a greater range of possibilities. Just as the introduction of metal skates in the late seventeenth century gave ice-skaters greater speed and mobility on the ice, so, a hundred years later, the first iron clubs began to add to the subtleties of golf. Then there was the introduction of the gutta-percha ball in the mid-nineteenth century (in place of the old cow-hide stuffed with a hatful of feathers) with its more controlled flight and longer life, and the game was set to take off on its international career.

The new methods of production that marked the Industrial and Agricultural Revolutions were not, of themselves, beneficial to sport, restricting both playing space and playing time, but very soon the steam power which was driving the looms was also being exploited in the interests of leisure. Steamboat trips down the Thames and the Clyde became popular jaunts - the trips to Margate and Ramsgate attracted 17,000 passengers in 1813, rising to no less than 105,000 by 1836. As well as providing this new recreational opportunity, steam power was also called upon to assist the maintenance and development of existing sports, and without it, indeed, the prize-ring would doubtless have sunk into obscurity much earlier than it did. But for the use of trains and river steamers in the 1840s and 1850s, the London base of the ring could hardly have existed. The Metropolitan police force was increasingly efficient, gentry support was thin, and crowd disorder such that promoters and fighters could seldom be certain of collecting any entrance money from spectators or of getting a fair, uninterrupted result to the bout. The hired river steamer and the private railway excursion seemed to be the answer to all the problems. The whole pugilistic party could be conveyed to a site of which few need have any foreknowledge, tickets for the transport could assure the promoters of an income, and price could be used to deter the less welcome.

It was, however, seldom as simple as it promised. Londoners round the docklands had an eye for paddle-steamers preparing themselves for a fight trip, and soon a whole string of craft, from coal barges to tug boats, would be carrying the 'cheapsiders' in the wake of the official fight vessel. Then there were often hazards in getting ashore at unfrequented spots, the tendency of the promoters to take their craft back after the one big fight they were interested in, ignoring any supporting contests, and then, very often, a late, slow haul up river, against both wind and tide. The railways looked a more attractive proposition, especially after Thomas Cook had unintentionally pointed the way by hiring special excursion trains. Earlier attempts to exploit the railway, using scheduled services, had been fraught with as many difficulties as river trips. They could be kept neither secret nor exclusive. Local police down the line could be warned by the new electric telegraph of the expected crowd, and once they had left their train all the passengers, gentry and plebs alike, were reduced to the ranks of pedestrians. Some of these excursions were certainly successful, with the various railway companies winning different reputations as providers - the favourite fighting line was the Eastern Counties, but the Great Western too often took the money without finding a safe site. The last great rail excursion was to the Sayers v Heenan fight in April, 1860, when two long special trains pulled out of London Bridge station at 4.00 am, took a deceptive, circuitous route, and landed their thousands in the Hampshire countryside. The police interfered in

The Great Western Railway - at Shrivenham Station (just after this print was made) fight followers disturbed the peace when they decamped here for the Broome v Terry fight in 1846.

the end, but by then the men had effectively had their contest, and an agreed draw was, by most, considered a fair settlement. By then, though, fight excursions had often been an occasion for crowd disorder at the London termini, with would-be passengers having to push their dangerous way through an aggressive mob. Most railway companies had refused to accept bookings, and when the *Regulation of Railways Act* of 1868 finally made the hiring of trains for fights illegal, they had in fact already virtually ceased, and the sport itself was in its long, slow dying.

The effects of the railways on horse-racing were much more positive, dramatic, and long-lasting. Once the railway arrived, the local race meeting changed its nature almost overnight. It became easier to travel daily to the races than to stay in town, the balls and assemblies disappeared, and what had been largely a social occasion became much more specifically a sporting meeting. The results could be even more drastic if the railway did *not* arrive. Some long-established fixtures disappeared from the Racing Calendar in mid-century often as a result of their isolation from the early railway network. Blandford, in Dorset, for example, had had its racing since the early 1600s, but when the South Western Railway reached Salisbury, some twenty miles away, in 1840, the Blandford meeting collapsed within a couple of years. Like other railway companies, the South Western was prepared to sponsor meetings served by its lines and Railway Stakes became a common feature of the racing programme.

It was not only spectators who were now moved more easily and rapidly. The same could apply to the horses. No longer did a long week-end have to be set aside to walk the horses from one course to another, and no longer did a horse's season have to be planned with a careful eye on the map and its round of regional meetings.

Major racecourses soon had their own railway stations. This one at Cheltenham is now derelict.

Newbury, however, is now enjoying a new lease of life.

Racing had for many years been the nearest the land possessed to a national sport, with most of the best horses meeting once a year at Newmarket, Epsom, or Doncaster. Now it was more completely so, and a horse could, in a single summer, race comfortably at York and Lincoln, at Brighton and Manchester, or wherever.

Cricket benefited likewise. The Hambledon players - who, in spite of legend, did not 'invent' the game but did dominate it for a few years in the later eighteenth century - had trundled along to their away games in a huge caravan-like wagon, at a few miles an hour. The new touring cricketers took the train and the game all over Britain, popularising it, and raising standards. National sport demanded national rules, and the easy communication offered by the railways made them simpler to achieve and maintain, in cricket and all other sports. Another uniformity brought by the railway was 'railway time,' to replace the local times that had made differences of up to half an hour between one part of the kingdom and another. By stringing their electric telegraph lines alongside their rails, the railways also made local news instantly available, and crowded London pubs no longer had to await the arrival of the carrier pigeon or the fastest horseman for the result of some distant fight or race. The impetus that this, in turn, gave to sports reporting was considerable - and for the pigeons it meant that their sporting future lay, with growing popularity, in racing.

Changes in attitudes towards time had other consequences for sport. The major racing events of the past, whether of men or horses, had always tended to be over long distances, measured in hours and even days for the humans and in heats of up to four miles for the horses. Attempts to time shorter, races, and thus establish standards for them were befogged by the absence of reliable stop-watches. The consequences can be seen in some of the claims made for earlier athletes, such as Mr Jollif who, having run a mile in five minutes in 1806, then undertook to run the same distance in four minutes, and to leap a given height at stated intervals! The result is not recorded, but it is reasonable to suppose that there is no distant record for the one-mile steeplechase still standing! With sharper time-keeping, though, there could be much more interest in shorter sprints, and in comparisons between one runner and another. Stop-watches also made their appearance on Newmarket Heath in the hands of trainers (and sly punters) just at the time when the fashion was moving away from long-distance hauls to shorter races run by younger, lighter horses.

In the second half of the nineteenth century technology was changing many aspects of the sporting scene. Mechanical turnstiles made sport more reliably remunerating by cutting out the odd light-fingered gate-keeper, and made the reporting of attendances much less dependent upon the wayward imaginations of the press. Concrete was in use in stadia by the end of the century, while the widespread use of rubber brought more efficient balls to any number of sports - it is little wonder that the age saw the popularity of several new ball games. There are many such instances where material advance was brought to the service of play. What did lag behind, though, was the application of scientific knowledge to the players themselves.

Medical science had made considerable progress by the early Victorian years - there was a greater awareness of hygienic needs, a concern for public health, and a modest recognition of the need for fresh air and exercise. The means to sporting fitness, however, were matters of considerable dispute, and not of much interest to the medical profession. The well-reported fight between the Tipton Slasher and the giant American, Freeman, was remarkable in many ways, and one of its novel features was that a leading London physician examined the two men to compare their potential as combatants, albeit with indeterminate results.

Training methods were hardly scientific and the physical fitness of sportsmen was often highly suspect. Pugilists had followed every sort of regime in their fight preparation, from a diet of raw meat and eggs (to make them savage, and strong in wind!) to running long distances, hopping and jumping, drinking sour buttermilk, and shadow boxing. During fights, swigs of brandy were common between rounds. For jockeys, weight reduction became more and more important with the move to lighter, younger horses, which also made more rides available to them, since a few gentlemen could make the 8½ stone limit. Jockeys began their slimming down programme some time before Easter, and usually took off 1 to 1½ stones in a week or ten days through savage dieting and exercise swathed in clothing - five or six waistcoats and two overcoats.

Boxers, by contrast, were usually corpulent men by today's standards, though with wrestling throws still allowed the added weight could be useful. They often continued to fight, too, into the veteran stage, with fighters like Joe Maddox, in his fifties, still taking on opponents half his age. Even chronic physical disability was no bar to pugilistic glory. Three of the greatest fighters of the early Victorian period all suffered from infirmities - Bendigo (William Thompson) was the nearest to being whole, with just the lingering lameness from an early knee injury. William Perry, the Tipton Slasher, had a congenitally deformed limb (a 'K' leg, in the language of the day) and James Bourke fought most his battles wearing a truss, was known as 'Deaf Bourke', and had a damaged knee which was always likely to fail in his later fights!

More so than with other sports, pugilism was a harsh, remorseless, and brutal game, taking to extremes the old common stresses on strength, endurance, and stamina, and making only modest demands on skill. One of the many reasons for the ring's demise was that it remained in this unreconstructed state, while other sports completed, during the Victorian years, the change of emphasis from sheer spectacle and conquest to fair and equal competition where the result was measured by something other than exhaustion and surrender. Training became more important, and trainers began to look to science, as technical ability became more important, and finesse in play became more admired. Scientific advances and technological innovation would be brought more and more into the service of sport, adding to its possibilities and, for the most part, making it a more acceptable activity.

The Middle Class and the Rediscovery of Play

The emergence of modern spectator sport in Britain took place against a background of steadily rising living standards during the hundred years following the 1770s. It was a prosperity, though, that was unevenly shared, and the upper levels of society benefited disproportionately. In particular, the middle classes grew in number, economic power, and social influence. As they became ascendant, they carried with them that complex of high, if sometimes hypocritical moral values known as 'Victorianism,' and for sport to find any place in the changing order it had to accommodate itself to these new values.

The Tipton Slasher
- William Perry

The upholders of the new morality came late and at first cautiously to the enjoyment of their own leisure. By the middle of the nineteenth century, though, they felt economically secure enough, and confident enough of their own status, to begin to assert their own right to play. It would need, however, to be play which did not involve the desertion of moral principle - healthy physical activity free from the sordid associations of the popular sports which, for generations, they had kept at such arm's length. They would not brook the old rowdiness, the drunken company, the brutality and the cruelty, the flouting of working hours, the inveterate gambling, the vice, crime and corruption in which sports had spent their earlier years.

It would be wrong to suggest that middle-class interest in sport was a totally novel phenomenon, even if it had only been a small minority of tradesmen and professional men who had been involved. In the few cases where the occupations of those arrested at prizefights are known, there was almost invariably a sprinkling of lawyers, commercial men, and tradesmen in the list. Sporting parsons continued to flourish through the first half of the nineteenth century, riding to hounds and even on the racecourse - one such was an Oxford cleric (under an assumed name) at the 1849 Cheltenham races. Such examples could be multiplied, but the broad brush picture remains largely true. There was little middle-class interest or, until the railway age, middle-class investment in sport. Such money as came into sport was from the more speculative edges of trade and commerce, from horse trading, carriage hire, innkeeping, money lending, and the like.

The universities of Oxford and Cambridge had discovered the delights of organised competitive sports by the 1830s, with their boat races, cricket matches, and even an annual billiards contest. By the mid-1840s it was becoming possible to admit to a taste for play, even, occasionally, at the expense of work, according to one commentator who had heard men say they never enjoyed sport as much 'as when stealing a day from the close application of business or professional exertion.' The difficulty remained of finding some proper sporting amusement. Of the three established sports, only cricket appeared to offer any real possibility of enlightened indulgence. Pugilism was obviously inappropriate. There might be a burst of interest in the doings of Tom Sayers in the late 1850s, and the city and stock exchange contributed generously to a fund raised for him after his fight with Heenan, but it was given on condition that he did not fight again. The respectable classes were drawing the final curtain on the old English sport. The racecourse, too, was no place for the scrupulous during its worst early Victorian years. It had to survive two parliamentary inquiries into gaming in the 1840s, and steady pressure locally from reforming interests. It remained under the domination of the landed classes, with financial support from those who could profit from meetings, the men in the horse trades, caterers and innkeepers, and the railway companies. The titles given to races indicate quite clearly who the turf's sponsors were.

While the reputable businessman or lawyer might allow himself an occasional visit to the local races, carefully segregating himself from the common throng with his grandstand ticket, the middle classes were not disposed to make much of the sport. Cricket held much greater possibilities for them. If it was aristocratic patronage that had launched cricket as a major sport, this had always been tempered by support from other classes. The list of members of the White Conduit Club (the effective forerunner of the MCC) in 1784 showed only a third of them with titles or military rank, and this process of dilution continued strongly with the MCC itself through the nineteenth century. It became a game dominated by middle-class members of clubs - and by middle-class morality. The abandoning of stake money, the campaign against gambling, the better control of crowds, the tightening of the practices and timing of games - all these fitted well with the demands of the new ethos.

Tom Sayers' tomb

They were symptomatic, too, of subtle changes that were taking place in the nature of spectator sport as a whole, bringing it into line with the changing expectations of what sport should offer, to both players and onlookers. It was, at its simplest, a change in taste from spectacle to competition. A zest for annihilation gave way to a taste for contention and emulation.

The prize ring was incapable of making concessions to the new styles. The fight to surrender would have to give way to a new code, with timed bouts and a measured result, before it could have any hope of revival. The racecourse took many decades to root out malpractice and could never escape the stigma of gambling, but in other respects racing had begun early to respond to the new mood by moving to shorter races with lighter horses. It achieved, too, a smarter timing as the century progressed and the railway began to demand that its excursion trains returned on schedule, and bookmakers were exposed to the telegraphed bet. Races at set times replaced the old casualness.

Cricket had much the easiest path to tread. The former practice of playing until a definite result was achieved had largely disappeared and - with more difficulty - even the hours of play were becoming more regularised. The greatest influence of the changing mood was to spell the eventual end of the road for the touring professional sides. While they had performed a great missionary task, what their matches usually lacked was any sense of equal competition, and the relish for seeing local heroes trounced by visiting giants eventually palled for both players and spectators alike. The growing importance of county matches from the middle of the century reflects the new desire for balanced contests, as well as having the appeal of local allegiance.

There were, too, other growing opportunities for the middle classes. A strong feature of Victorian sport was its tendency to become more strictly class orientated than the play of the past. In some instances it was a question of economic discrimination. Yachting demanded financial resources available only to the few, however much pleasure it might bring to spectators starved of other entertainment. Rowing could be more accessible, and the regattas, numerous from the early part of the century, were at first open to all - amateurs and professionals, men and women. This gradually changed. The professionals and the ladies were relegated to subsidiary and often near-comic events, and then excluded altogether. Shooting rested primarily on land ownership and was in essence an exclusive sport. Loud claims might be voiced for the democratic nature of the National Rifle Association which brought both masters and gamekeepers together, but woe betide any other unlucky plebeian caught taking shots at game. Even fishing began to sharpen its class divisions. Railway excursions took their loads of London artisans down to the Sussex rivers for coarse fishing (arousing Sabbatarian complaints because they did so on Sundays), but the richer pickings of the trout and salmon streams were ever more jealously protected by landlords. Hunting, too, underwent the same transformation. The old heterogeneous collection of local workers' hunts were gradually whittled away, and the opportunities for others to hunt their land were suppressed, partly because the gentry hunts began to meet on more days of the week than in the past, partly as a consequence of this growing sense of separateness which was pushing the recreation of the different classes steadily further apart.

It was the completely new sports, though, which took on a characteristic middle-class flavour. Climbing the Alps, for instance, became a regular possibility after the coming of the railway. It admirably suited bourgeois sporting requirements, with its undoubted healthiness, its strenuous physical exertion, its proper sting of danger to try the moral fibre - and its exclusiveness. Billiards was far from being a new sport - a version of it was as old as Shakespeare's *Antony and Cleopatra* - but it had a new vogue as an upper-class parlour game, with the billiard room a prerequisite in any house with pretensions to grandeur. As a public sport, its associations with gambling and disorder had led to the shutting-down of billiards and bagatelle rooms earlier in the century. Its revival as an after-dinner game for the gentry is still reflected in the dress of the professional snooker player - the evening attire, with the jacket removed.

Another game with a strong domestic base was croquet, and again it demanded a certain level of affluence, enough to provide for a large garden and a lawn. Its progress was aided, as attitudes towards middle-class recreation became more relaxed, by its availability to both ladies and gentlemen. Indeed, the search for lost balls in the bushes gave a rare unchaperoned opportunity for mild play of another sort - and a regular topic for *Punch* cartoons. The other up-and-coming sports of the later nineteenth century - tennis, badminton, cycling, and golf - also, sooner or later, gave play opportunities to women as well as men, while a garden game like croquet had other advantages that were soon replicated elsewhere. High hedges meant that play could take place at will, even on the otherwise forbidden Sabbath. The company, too, would be invited, and therefore selective. They were, in miniature, the conditions that would prevail in the private sports club, the essential organisation through which the growing world of middle-class sport would come to preserve and promote its exclusivity.

The rebirth of middle-class play can rightly be seen as essentially selfish. However, and if largely by accident, it turned out to be much more than that. It was, in fact, through the impetus it gave to the resurrection and revival of the old game of football, the trigger for the growth of the one great working-class sport of the next century or more, one that was to take over virtually the whole of the sporting globe.

Saturdays - Soccer Days
In the last quarter of the nineteenth century, the leisure activities of the bulk of the population were at last brought into correspondence again with their working lives, and the massive changes in the social order of the past one hundred years at length found their expression in the people's leisure pursuits. Whereas much popular sport had taken place in spite of the prevailing attitudes and actions of the establishment, now it could hope to find a measure of approval.

All sports shared to a greater or lesser extent in the sea change. The key, though, to the new sporting world lay with football, at first a surprising candidate for innovation and leadership. It had little history of spectating, it was noted as being in decline as a game of the streets and the fields, and had no social status, a pursuit for boys and youths, and the rougher ones at that. On the other hand, these very elements did leave football free from the inherited taints of gambling and stake money, and all the sins and malpractices that they implied. All it had to loose was its basic disorder, its lack of agreed form. Those who took the first steps to remedy the game's anarchy had little idea of the sort of egg they were hatching, nor did any of the contemporary commentators. Had the Old Etonians

The Village Ba' Game by Duncan Carse 1818 (Dundee Art Galleries and Museums)

been aware that, scarcely before the third quarter of the century was out, they would be beaten to the FA Cup by players from Blackburn, the history of the sport might have been altogether different.

Two elements came fortuitously together to give impetus to football's rise. On the one hand, there was its adoption by the growing public schools as the standard winter game. On the other, there was the availability of a free Saturday afternoon throughout the year, and the need for some winter pursuit to occupy it.

As late as 1850, there were few signs of what the next quarter of a century was to hold. The game - or, rather, the several games - was beginning to play a notable part in the recreation of public schoolboys. Meanwhile, outside the schools, there were some stirrings of organisation and occasional hints of a game which might take over from the mass communal contests and the informal street play, both of which were under pressure. For their part, the schools were more concerned to establish their own identities than to find a common game form. Indeed, the facilities, or lack of them, could dictate the nature of the play. Westminster School had to suffer football in the cloisters, only finally banned some ten years after the school had acquired playing space in Tothill Fields, a former popular sporting ground in rougher days. By 1841 there were signs of organisation there - 11-a-side matches between the rowers and the rest. Eton had its own versions in the occasionally played wall game and the more usual field game, while both Harrow and Rugby had their quite firm codes, the one with a bias towards kicking, the other more tolerant of handling.

The first hint of some reconciliation between the different practices of the individual schools grew out of the wish of former pupils to go on playing when they reached university. In the early 1840s, men from Eton, Shrewsbury, and Winchester played on Parker's Piece in Cambridge to rules which still survive in a later version, and which point to a catching and kicking game, whose nearest school equivalent was Harrow's. It was a sure sign that football was escaping from its image as a game for the rough-and-ready once young gentlemen could find it reasonable to enjoy it after their schooldays were over. But the public schools did not invent football. What the schools and their products did achieve, and as much by accident as design, was a measure of uniformity in a long-played winter game, widespread and still popular, even in its doldrum days. They would eventually reduce the infinity of local varieties of play into two major forms. Moreover, just as Oxbridge graduates had once played their part in the spread of cricket, they were, in turn, to aid the diffusion of the two forms of football over the whole of the land, and even beyond. The rapid growth of football, though, was only possible because the popular zest for a kicking and throwing ball game was deeply ingrained, and remained still alive. The streets of industrial towns such as Bolton, Sheffield, Nottingham, and the rest, had never completely lost the game, in spite of the best efforts of policemen and prosecutors.

By the early 1860s it had become popular enough with young adults, many of them products of the public schools, for an appreciable number of clubs to be formed, most of the more organised being in the south. With them came further attempts to bring some communality into the game. Cambridge, through its Trinity men from the public schools, produced another version of its rules in 1863, and later in the same year came the decisive meeting of a group of southern clubs at the Freemason's Tavern in London. It was this meeting, on 26 October

1863, which led to the foundation of the Football Association. With the exception of Blackheath, all the clubs happened to be followers of the kicking, catching, and dribbling game. The crucial element in their new rules was accordingly the ban on running with the ball. Although the rules were in other respects made as catholic as possible, this prohibition was bound to be unpalatable to those loyal to the Rugby style of play. After some hesitation, these clubs went their own way, the split confirmed by the setting up of the Rugby Football Union in 1871. The distinction between the kicking and handling codes did not, however, appear at the time to be conclusive. Some clubs were, at first, prepared to play under either set of rules and *The Times* of 1872, for instance, was still publishing reports of both styles under the common heading of 'football,' often not making clear which match was which.

Meanwhile, the geographical growth of the organised game had been rapid, Sheffield and Nottingham leading the way, quickly followed by other industrial towns in the North and Midlands. This was no mere chance. By another of the fortuitous coincidences which marked the game's early years, the industrial workers found that they had free time to play on the very occasion which the public schoolboys had always been accustomed to use - Saturday afternoon. From the eighteenth century the schools had always seen Wednesday and (particularly) Saturday afternoons as their playing times and the new clubs had taken to Saturday games from the start. This was quite foreign to all the leisure traditions of the artisan classes, for whom Saturdays had been, if anything, the most hectic days of the week, in a late attempt to boost the pay packet. Since the mid-1840s, though, there had been a steady extension of early Saturday afternoon closing in the factories. It was a patchy and piecemeal process, varying not only from place to place, but also from trade to trade, but by the 1870s a government commission was describing the practice as 'almost universal' in industry.

Until the advent of football, little advantage had been taken of this new free time in the towns, with pedestrianism being the only sport to shift some of its emphasis away from the traditional Mondays or Tuesdays. *The Times* of 1861, for example, was complaining that the working classes of Blackburn spent their Saturday afternoons at singing rooms ('where depravity prevails and morality is at a low ebb') and then went off to the beer shops. This was the recreational vacuum which the Blackburn football clubs would fill. The spread of football out from the London area followed almost exactly the growth of the free Saturday afternoon. In the first year of the Football League, 1888/9, there were only three teams from outside the factory heartlands of provincial soccer, Lancashire and greater Birmingham. The three 'outsiders' were Derby, Notts County and Stoke, and they finished up in the bottom three places.

It has been suggested that regular spectator sport could not have begun earlier than it did because of the absence of disposable income among potential customers. This is questionable, considering the flourishing state of the licensing trade throughout the middle years of the century, though it was certainly the case that the prestige workers, those who benefited most from the prosperity of the 1860s, were available in numbers where the new game first flourished. The experience of individual towns is instructive. Liverpool, for instance, was slow to achieve wholesale Saturday afternoon closing, the middle classes and the more favoured industrial workers winning their freedom well in advance of the mass of the population, and this has been argued as the reason for the dominance of cricket there (as a more elite game) and the late arrival of football.

Clubs in the South were originally largely made up of former public schoolboys. Those in the Midlands and North were more diverse in their origins. Frequently the leadership came from the same source, often from clergymen, who could now support popular play, as it was no longer virtually synonymous with either labour indiscipline or sabbath-breaking. The club could also spring from the workplace (such as West Bromwich, from the Albion Works), or from some other community of sporting interest - Sheffield United provided a winter game for the club's cricketers. Grammar schools provided some clubs (such as Blackburn Rovers, aided by a group of Old Malvernians) and even, on occasion, Board Schools did the same - Droop Street School in Kentish Town was the inspiration behind Queen's Park Rangers, now moved to Shepherd's Bush. Even an esoteric event such as a tripe supper could produce a football club, as happened at Middlesbrough.

Counties followed the national example and set up their own County Football Associations, each soon with its own County Cup. These trophies, along with the FA Cup itself, provided the only occasions for formal competition for some twenty years, until the establishment of the Football League took the game into a new and very different phase. Meanwhile, the expansion of football had quickly over-reached country boundaries. The players on Queen's Park, one of Glasgow's public open spaces, formed a club in 1867, and were soon competing not only with other Scottish teams, but also making their mark in the English FA Cup, where they were exempt until the semi-final in the first competition, partly because of the cost of travel. When the Scottish FA launched their own cup in 1874, Queen's Park were the first winners. The Welsh Cup followed four years later, won first by Wrexham. The game developed on a scale and at a pace that was new to sport. International matches between England and Scotland began in 1870, when the Scottish eleven was very much a scratch Anglo-Scot combination, but within a matter of fifteen years all the home associations were playing against each other, fielding truly representative teams.

The handling code was slower to form its own associations - the Rugby Football Union dates from 1871 - but within only a few months an English team was playing its first international against Scotland. In the following year, the trio of conspicuous annual Oxbridge contests was completed with the mounting of the first University rugby game, half a century after the rowing and cricket matches between Oxford and Cambridge had originally pointed the distant way to this wholly new style of sporting competition.

The coming of football as a large-scale sport, and by the last decades of the century it had reached that status, was not the start of the revolution in sporting practice which took place during the Victorian age, but was, rather, its culmination. The gradual change in taste from spectacle and submission to balanced competition, from playing for stake money or wagers to play for the sport's own sake, was one that had had its first manifestations in the otherwise inexplicable popularity of the University Boat Race from the mid-century onwards, when it and the University cricket match began to draw in thousands of spectators and arouse great press interest. The change had produced modes of play which, for all their general acceptability, still posed their questions, especially in a tendency to classlessness, which could have a threat of social anarchy about it. And if money considerations had disappeared in one form, they were soon threatening to appear in another.

Headmasters, Gentlemen, and Players

The education system of Victorian England was an exact expression of its class structure, constantly reinforcing that structure in many areas of life, not least in the type of play it allowed and promoted.

The British public school - for what began in England soon had its exemplars over the whole kingdom - was a powerful agent in the development of those sporting styles which came to predominate in the last years of the century, but it was far from seeking to create a scheme of popular play which could threaten the whole social order. The schools served the expanding middle classes, particularly in their upper commercial and professional reaches, producing men who could oversee not only the country's continued prosperity but could also administer the world's largest, ever-expanding empire. They sought to inculcate such qualities as manliness, strength, loyalty, discipline and powers of leadership, and arrived at a convinced philosophy that games, especially team games, were an ideal medium through which to achieve these character-moulding ends.

Individual schools had originally taken various routes towards this common ethos of athleticism. In the first place, games had helped to rescue the great boarding schools from their pre-Victorian anarchy, when remorseless beatings on the one hand had been met with riot, rebellion, and lock-outs on the other. The sporting lives of the pupils then had centred on the hunting of frogs, rabbits, squirrels, and anything else that moved, and they were given to wandering out of control over all the surrounding countryside. Their play, like much of that of the common people, seemed to belong to a barbarous age that should have been left behind. Games that were nearer to the acceptable were being played, but they were seldom central to the school's activities. Some schools were playing cricket or rowing against each other, or had their own recognised football styles, and it was on these foundations that the new sporting curriculum was to be built. This was to be achieve largely by way of infiltration, encouraging the more organised forms of play, providing facilities, and gradually corralling the young onto the playing field. What had been an embarrassment to headmasters became their pride.

One factor in the success of the schools in the updating and upgrading of their recreational life was the existence already, in the 1830s and 1840s, of a generation of graduates from Oxford and Cambridge who had had some experience of organised competitive sport. Cricket and rowing contests between the two universities were eventually followed by those in other sports until, by the end of the century there were over twenty such, including racquets, steeplechasing, athletics, golf, tennis, polo, boxing, swimming, and - one of the earliest - billiards. The progress of athleticism was self-perpetuating. The athletic undergraduates from the schools extended and strengthened the hold of sports on the universities, and returned as teachers, even more strongly convinced of the rightness of their competitive muscular stance.

It was all so different in working-class education. Such play as their station in life justified could be left to chance outside school hours. Physical training, in the elementary schools, was confined to drill. The officers needed troops who would be dutifully regimented and led, and their wives needed domestics trained in obedience. There was little by way of sports or other regularly organised recreational activities in the state educational system until after the First World War.

The sharp distinctions of childhood were progressively strengthened in adult sporting experience. The class divisions of Victorian Britain found one of their many expressions in the line that was gradually more firmly drawn between the amateur player and the rest. For all the claims that it was a rejection of the notion of financial gain from sport, it was much more than that - it was an assertion of the immutability of the class system.

The whole history of cricket before the abolition of the distinction between amateurs and players in the 1960s demonstrates this. Until well into the nineteenth century gentlemen cricketers had no qualms over taking their profits from stake money and side-bets on their play, and usually stood to make much more than their professionals. The cricketer to profit most from the Victorian game was undoubtedly W.G. Grace, whose expenses always included the cost of a locum for his practice and whose claret bill on tour was, according to Arthur Shrewsbury, itself larger than what a professional cost for the whole trip. Shrewsbury's own case indicates that the distinction was social rather than financial - as a highly successful businessman, he was certainly wealthier than many of the amateurs with whom he played.

Cricket, was indeed a game which by its very nature lent itself to a division of labour and status between master and servant, and all the more so after the introduction of round-arm and then over-arm bowling made this a more strenuous pursuit. The gentlemen were predominantly the batsmen, the players the bowlers, a distinction usually evident in all the long history of the annual Gentlemen v. Players matches. Briefly, in the decades of the autonomous touring teams in mid-century, there had been some threat that the paid men might take over the running of the game. However, as their appeal faded and the county match became the staple ingredient of cricket, the MCC and the county committees took a firm grip on the players - economic pressures kept them firmly in their place and regulations effectively tied a player to one employer through stringent birth or residential qualifications.

If cricket's answer to the problem of accommodating the lower orders was through a division of labour and an emphasis on differentiated status, other sports had to look to other solutions. There was some logic in making discriminations in sports which, for some contestants, might correspond closely to their everyday paid employment. Rowing was the prime case, calling on the same skills and strengths as the waterman used in his job. When gentlemen made a sport of rowing towards the end of the eighteenth century, it was reasonable enough that they should not pit themselves against professional boatmen, but as class consciousness grew more acute, even the usual happy mix of events in regattas, with races for fishermen, watermen and other working groups along-side the gentry contests came to be rejected, and the amateurs went further and further into the indefensible to preserve their exclusivity. Their ensuing definition of 'professional' then went far beyond the exclusion of paid watermen - it excluded all who earned, or ever had earned a living from manual labour. It was a fatuous distinction which excluded the postman and the policeman, but allowed in the post office clerk, and among the more notable of the rejected was the father of Princess Grace of Monaco! Even when the Amateur Rowing Association at last changed its extreme stance in 1937, it still barred any oarsman whose employment was in any way connected with boats, whether or not they had raced for money prizes, and this generations after the waterman's trade had effectively disappeared. At length, in 1956, modernity almost caught up with the oarsmen when they finally limited their definition of professionalism to rowing for money.

The example of rowing was exceptional only in its extravagance. The exclusion of the professional, excused on the twin grounds of making for equal competition and avoiding corruption, had its varying influence on all sports. The Amateur Athletic Association followed the pattern set by rowing in its first rules in 1865, excluding both professional performers *and* 'any tradesman, mechanic, artisan, or labourer.' There was certainly some initial need to give status to amateur athletics by cutting it off completely from the wholesale disrepute of pedestrianism, but such exclusivity soon threatened the new sport with disintegration and within a few years the AAA limited its prohibition to those who had actually competed for money. Unlike the athletes, the golfers succeeded in grafting the new exclusivity on to the existing sport, without any sharp break from the past. Paid caddies and greenkeepers played against amateurs and the Open Championship at first had money prizes which gentlemen had no qualms about accepting. This situation only altered towards the end of the century, as the game became more anglicised, and the entries of any who had taken money prizes began to be refused by the organisers of amateur competitions.

Where games were designed primarily for the players themselves and gave little heed to the amusement of onlookers, the pro-am distinction was a useful means of maintaining their class status, and the private club, with its control over membership, further protected their exclusivity. Where, on the other hand, sports began to attract spectators, accepted them, made provision, and integrated their gate money into the economics of the sport, its administrators found themselves in a dilemma. Themselves virtually all men of the middle classes, few had much enthusiasm for professionalism in sport, though those in the Midlands and the North tended to be less given to elitist views than those of the more traditional South. As they invested in grounds and facilities, however rudimentary, they began to welcome spectators, and these, for their part wanted both entertainment and success. It became important for such clubs not just to have players who enjoyed playing the game, but to have players who played it well. Many of the best players, though, could not afford to keep taking time off from their regular work without some financial recompense. From recouping what they lost, it was a short step to paying them more money for playing than they were losing by not working, and then inducing players to come to a club - and in football this was usually from Scotland - by the offer of a good job. As many officials were large employers this was usually easy to manage.

After protests over the appearance of professional players in the early 1880s (Preston were expelled from the FA Cup in 1884 on this account) and then a threatened breakaway by the Lancashire clubs, the Football Association accepted a form of professionalism. It was a cautious and tightly controlled measure drawn up by its secretary, F.W. Alcock, who also happened to be secretary of Surrey County Cricket Club and made full use of cricket's long experience of defining - and confining - the professional's role. The other football code, in its turn, went through the same traumas over the payment of players, but with a quite different outcome. The southern clubs were firmly opposed to northern enthusiasms for league competitions and the taking of gate money. These were characterising rugby in Yorkshire and Lancashire just as they had come to characterise soccer. At a meeting in London, conscientiously packed by southern representatives, the Rugby Football Union threw out proposals for limited professionalism in the game. In 1895, the larger northern clubs, already committed to the spectator-orientated game, went their own way and formed the Northern Rugby Football Union.

The founding of the Rugby League, as it became known, was the most prominent manifestation of a deep divide in attitudes which went far beyond discrimination between amateur and professional sport. The ethos of the southern sporting establishment, given over unreservedly to the cult of athleticism, remained, at heart, at odds with the grass roots play of the broad mass of the industrial population. It is a divide which still leaves its scars, including a tradition of sports history which neglects, for instance, the league cricket played by thousands of teams in the Midlands and the North for the best part of a century, and gives rugby league football little more than a footnote compared with its treatment of the union game.

The Rugby Union's attitude towards its rebellious rival has always held a peculiar mixture of obscurantism and snobbery. Until recently, the numerous amateur rugby league players (who far outnumber the professionals) were technically barred from the precincts of union clubs. The continuing barriers erected by the rugby unions against professionalism eventually tumbled with a breathless rapidity which found the home union officials very much on the back foot and leaves both codes in a state of flux which it will take the new century to sort out.

The Living Past V

Although we know a great deal about organised Victorian sport, particularly from its later years, there is a surprising amount of play over which we remain comparatively ignorant. There was much happening in working-class recreation, as we know from a few studies already done, which remains still unearthed, and related to this is the growing awareness of local and regional variety, which further enquiries will doubtless strengthen.

The diversity that begins to appear in sport from this time forward makes it possible to give only partial suggestions as to topics for local study. In horse-racing, for instance, while there were numerous new meetings started, most were short-lived - of 99 to begin in the 1860s, only 50 lasted for five years, and a mere 24 for ten. Why were they set up, and why did they fail? They could arise from the influence of a powerful patron, as at Mansfield, where the Duke of Portland developed a long-disused but still recognisable course (now a recreation ground, but still known as the Racecourse), or could result from the enterprise of publicans and tradesmen, or even the direct sponsorship of a railway company. They could fail from social and moral pressure, financial shortcomings, or even the poor quality of the racing. Only by much local searching shall we find where the balance lay.

Similarly, the broad national consequences of such events as the coming of the railways and the winning of the free Saturday afternoon are well known, but their local implications have been only patchily explored. Their effects were staggered over some fifty years, and their impact differed from place to place. Advertisements in the local press and surviving posters will often reveal sporting excursions on the recently arrived railway. As to the Saturday early closing, an example of some of its sporting repercussions can be found in Nottingham, which lay between the extremes of industrial liberality and restraint. In 1861, the hosiery workers, in the city's first industry, had largely traded off their occasional holidays for fairs and races for a free afternoon. Sports clubs appeared almost at once. Nottingham Rowing Club was founded the next year and Nottinghamshire County Football Club soon followed, as did Nottingham Forest a little later, set up by the clients of the Clinton Arms. The progress, though, towards a full free afternoon was somewhat halting and it was another decade or more before it extended to the lace warehouses, the city's other major manufacturing product. The Nottingham picture itself needs painting in more detail, and an analysis of what happened in all towns and cities is much needed.

Moreover, the concentration of attention has been predominantly on *urban* sport. Poverty and the absence of leisure time undoubtedly restricted the sporting opportunities of the rural worker, particularly, for instance, in East Anglia and the South West, where there was no substantial competition from industry. Again there is need for much more systematic local study of how the available free time was spent in these areas.

History may never quite repeat itself, but an awareness of current issues in their historical dimension can add to our appreciation of the present. Travelling to sports events has caused concern ever since at least the 1625 Sunday Observance Act, with its ban on moving out of the home parish for play. Past and present attempts to control sporting travellers are well worth considering in the light of recent problems with football supporters. Technical advances continue to have profound and rapid influences on sports of all sorts. This not only applies to sports where the machine is central to the performance, such as motor-racing, yachting, or bob-sleighing. It also has more subtle effects - the introduction of the plastic-covered ball in football, the fibre-glass vaulting pole, new safety measures, and so on. In cricket, for instance, short-pitched bowling would surely have been outlawed had not helmets and specialised padding become available to give some protection to batsmen.

From the later Victorian age, there are many surviving sporting structures, though they are always in danger of demolition. Good photographic records of disappearing public baths, racecourse grandstands and the course's station, strange phenomena like fives walls, old cricket grounds - all are needed, and needed in a manner which brings out as much of their sporting significance as possible. Searches among old postcards and photographs can also uncover occasional gems, as can illustrations in contemporary newspapers towards the end of the century.

Novels, essays, and biographies also have their insights. Thackeray, for instance, had an abiding interest in the sporting scene of his youth, while both Hazlitt and George Borrow have dramatic accounts of prize-fights. While sport was not generally foremost in the minds of Victorian novelists, such instances can be multiplied. The historical study of sport also becomes much richer from this period. Its background can be studied in Harold Perkin, *The Origin of Modern English Society 1780-1880* (London and Toronto, 1969), and, focusing more closely on sport, Peter Bailey, *Leisure and Class in Victorian England*

(London, Toronto and Buffalo, 1978), James Walvin, *Leisure and Society* (London, 1978), and John Lowerson and John Myerscough, *Time to Spare in Victorian England* (Brighton, 1977). For the establishment and influence of the new athleticism, there is J.A. Mangan, *Athleticism in the Victorian and Edwardian Public School* (Cambridge, 1981), and for the impact of new means of travel there is useful information in J.A.R. Pimlott, *The Englishman's Holiday: A Social History* (London, 1947), and Alan Delgado, *The Annual Outing and other Excursions* (London, 1977). The fullest and most penetrating work on soccer in the period is Tony Mason, *Association Football and English Society* (Brighton, 1980), while the FA's own *History of the Football Association* (London, 1953) is a useful if unexciting reference source.

6

Edwardians and After

The twentieth century, which began in hope and optimism, was scarred within a lifetime by two world wars. Sport, however, continued to colonise new territories, to find new forms, to draw in greater numbers, and, eventually, to attract ever-greater popular participation.

The actuality of the Edwardian sporting world, so shattered by the events of 1914 to 1918, is hard to rediscover. It tends to exist in a dream-like vision perpetuated by modern film makers of constant summer sunshine, of endless blue skies, with lithe flannelled youths playing graceful cricket on immaculate turf, their parasolled ladies in decorous attendance. It is a picture, alas, that never had more than the most partial and superficial relationship with the Edwardian realities. If Joseph Strutt, aided by the harshness of the Industrial Revolution, had created a gloomy view of early nineteenth-century sport, it was nostalgic autobiographers and rhapsodic sports commentators who did much to construct the Edwardian idyll. The greatest of the sporting journalists, the lyrical Neville Cardus, could write that the sport of his youth 'comes back to mind as though lighted by eternal sunshine' - and that was just Old Trafford, in smoky Manchester. Not by chance was he also his newspaper's music correspondent! Looking back, through the filtering horrors of a World War, this vision certainly belonged to a lost world, but it did not have to be a perfect one. It could hardly be so, even in its play, in an era when, if profits soared, real wages declined, when trades unionists and suffragettes were alike ground down and had to campaign bitterly for their causes.

The immediate expectations of the British people after 1918 did begin again in hope and expectation. They looked for the land fit for heroes that they had been promised. The anticipation gradually withered, and the General Strike of 1926 finally signalled the end of all confidence in a more open and equal society. What had been won was greater leisure, with the significant reductions in working hours during the first two years of peace, but for the rest of the inter-war period any added freedom from labour was to arise much more from unemployment and short-time working than from any benevolence. Moreover, much of the liberality of wartime play was lost, particularly the relaxation that had been enjoyed over Sunday sport.

In spite of all the constraints, though, the twenties and thirties did see both steady growth in the traditional summer and winter games and also a widening participation in sports of every kind by more and more of the population. In particular, the sporting horizons of women at last began to be raised. By and large, it was a process which gradually seeped down the social scale, upper-class women being its first beneficiaries, but it did embrace the sports of the masses, such as darts, as well as those of the very few, such as Channel swimming. Throughout the first three decades of the century football particularly increased its hold on the affections and enthusiasms of the bulk of the population - if cricket had been *England's* national game in 1900, there can be little question that football, in one or other of its codes, had become *Britain's* major sporting pursuit by the 1920s and 1930s.

The Edwardian Summer

The upper and middle classes certainly enjoyed their Edwardian prosperity, but they enjoyed it at greater and greater distance from the rest of the people. Their sport became ever more separate from that of the working classes. Tennis and golf, for instance, both flourished as never before, but largely as enclosed sports (Scottish golf was an exception) with high social barriers built round the private clubs to preserve their exclusivity. There were few public facilities for either game in most parts of the kingdom. The only role for the worker was as club servant - there were over 20,000 greenkeepers and others on the payroll of golf clubs when the 1912 National Insurance Act caused consternation by requiring clubs to contribute 3d a week for each of their paid caddies, who in turn had 4d deducted from their weekly wages. So far as the golfing professional was concerned, his status was peculiar. He was usually less firmly discriminated against than paid performers in other sports - it has been suggested that a parallel would be found in fencing, with its 'professors' - but the clubs themselves tended towards an ever tighter clannishness. Jews, for instance, thwarted by their failure to be accepted elsewhere, responded by forming their own clubs.

Cycling presented another mix of the class issues which bedevilled late Victorian and Edwardian sport and recreation. At first, the cost of cycles had meant that cycling was predominantly a middle-class pursuit. By the 1890s, however, higher wages and lower costs had opened up the activity to at least the more affluent of the artisan classes and it rapidly became the great recreation of a broad social range. The Cyclists' Touring Club boasted 60,000 members by the turn of the century, doubtless the largest sporting organisation in the world. As a spectator sport, cycling's growth had been spectacular, and had extended its social appeal still wider. Road and track races had pulled in the crowds from their earliest days, and the gravel track at the Crystal Palace had been laid down as early as 1869. Races were mounted in such diverse settings as the Agricultural Hall, Islington (most famed, in sporting terms, for its marathon six-day pedestrian races), Headingly Cricket Ground, Leeds, with its banked track, and Trent Bridge.

The status of cycling was further complicated by its readiness to accept professionals and the general support of manufacturers. This was troublesome of itself to the purists, and more problems arose because mixed athletics and cycling meetings were common. The increasingly ambiguous status of competitive cycling was, though, only one reason for the decline in popularity of the pursuit as a whole during the early years of the present century. Other debilitating factors were also at work, much like those which had brought pedestrianism into disrepute half a century earlier - the attraction of the Crystal Palace became sullied by fixed races, the exorbitant fees demanded by professionals, and the difficulty of defining amateurism in a sport tied to the cycling manufacturers. Then there was the attraction of other new sports, such as indoor skating, then enjoying one of its several bursts of popularity.

If the Edwardians relished their newer sports, they also looked more benignly on one of the oldest, horse-racing. When the Prince of Wales' Persimmon won the Derby in 1893 the final seal of respectability was accorded the turf. Control over its affairs had become progressively tighter. Gambling could not be outlawed, but it had been made more honest. The rougher London courses had been closed by statute, and under new Jockey Club rules at least £300 of added prize money had to be available for each day's racing, courses had to conform to new demands on lay-out, and the licensing of new meetings was strictly controlled. The need for greater financial backing reduced the number of second-rate courses, and the old system of open access began to give way to paid admission after the opening of Sandown, Kempton, and other 'Park' courses, commercially run as joint stock companies, in the 1870s. The railway now brought virtually all the surviving courses (many with their own stations) within reach of large population centres. Order improved, not merely as a result of moral effort, but as a consequence of paid entrance and the considerable property interests that course owners sought to protect.

The racing of horses remained closer to the British heart than the racing of human beings, and athletics was still providing little more than a footnote to the sporting story. London provided a home for the 1908 Olympics, but it was solely as a result of Rome's default, and the presence of the royal family was a much stronger crowd-puller than the athletes themselves, with acres of empty grandstands whenever royalty was absent. The one unforgettable image of these games is of the exhausted and half-conscious Dorando Pietri being illegally helped to the tape at the end of the marathon. The special medal subsequently presented to him by the queen underlines his standing in the popular mind as the one real hero of the whole proceedings. The assistance given to Pietri, though, was just one example of the irregularities that marked these games, which were the last at which the home country was allowed to provide all the officials. They contributed little to international goodwill (many would suggest that this was not unique among Olympic meetings) and Anglo-American rivalry in particular was marked, embittered by the Irish ancestry of many of the trans-Atlantic competitors. Awkward questions were also raised over sponsored cyclists and 'shamateur' tennis players.

The sporting self-image was not much disturbed by such short-comings. The peculiar genius of the place and the times was held not to lie in such fringe trivialities as athletics, cycling, or lawn tennis, but in what was accepted as the national sport. Cricket had become *the* English game. Its development during the second half of the Victorian age had been the usual sporting mix of accident and design. For a generation or more the game had been so dominated by the professional touring sides that at one time even the hegemony of the MCC appeared to be threatened. County matches, though, which had for long been part of cricket, proved in the end to be more to new sporting tastes than the old touring spectaculars, and county clubs were established on a permanent basis. They began to prosper, both from increasing membership and rising gate money. The professional cricketer might sometimes regret his loss of independence - Arthur Shrewsbury never lost his suspicion of 'committee cricket' - but in return he began to have some security, modest as it might be. Even wealthier counties such as Surrey paid no more than 30/- to £2 a week during the season, and a retainer of £1 (30/- for a few) in winter. The prospect of perhaps doubling the summer wage with tips for bowling at members in the nets, and the distant hope of a benefit after ten or a dozen years' service, still hardly made it a full-time paying job. The benefit itself was such a speculative venture that some professionals would not risk being landed with its expenses if rain ruined the takings.

Cricket managed to become the national game in spite of the fact that only a third of the counties were recognised as 'first class' and thus in contention for the country championship. The championship itself was an invention of the press years before it had its official rules, and even these faced difficulties that are still not resolved today. In the years between 1890 and 1914, there were four different schemes for allocating points, and so deciding league placings, and there have been several others since. How to evaluate drawn matches remains the problem, one unknown, for instance, to major league baseball, with its clear win or lose outcomes. The championship remains as an interesting anachronism in the geographical sense, a visible sign of the conservatism of sporting habits. Some counties such as Middlesex, Worcestershire, and Yorkshire, after nearly a quarter of a century of local government reorganisation, now exist *only* as cricket teams, though a new local government review in the 1990s could well see them restored to the political map. Meanwhile Yorkshire has finally deserted its tradition of playing only men born within its (now non-existent!) boundaries and expects to have an overseas player in 1992.

The county set-up did still have rivals to contend with after the touring sides had had their day. The industrial areas of the Midlands and the North proved strong enough in talent and resources to accommodate both county cricket and a flourishing pattern of league cricket and 'money matches', but elsewhere there was a more serious threat from country-house cricket. This phenomenon, around the turn of the century, provided a strong counter-attraction to the best amateurs who might understandably prefer a week-end in one of the great houses of the aristocracy to a week-end at Bramall Lane or Edgbaston. For the well-mannered amateur, with some talent for the game, half the summer could be pleasantly occupied moving from one sumptuously fêted event to the next. Here the play was more important than the result. It was the gentleman's answer to the new vulgar competitiveness of leagues and championships, now extending itself into even the greenest of shires with the advent of the Minor Counties competition in 1895 - predictably opposed at the time by the MCC. The most influential leaders of the game, though, such as Lord Hawke, lent their considerable weight to the county game, setting examples which the best of the other amateurs found hard to oppose. Country-house cricket became the resort of the second-rate and finally died, with so much else of the Edwardian world, in the grime and blood of Flanders.

Great stress was laid on the grace and beauty of cricket. Its aesthetic and its ethic went hand in hand. Paradoxically, though, these first years of the new century saw the game becoming much more methodical and systematic, much more of a percentage performance than an exercise in elegance. Bowlers became more accurate, and batsmen, in turn, became more resourceful. The great players of the past had traditionally been off-side strikers of the ball, and leg-side hitting was frowned upon as rustic, if not actually unfair. C.B. Fry recalled that in his schooldays he was taught that it was ill-mannered to hit the ball to areas where no fielder was placed - a thesis which, incidentally, never gained much currency north of the Trent! It was there that such bowlers as Rhodes and Hurst achieved the consistency that obliged batsmen to take runs wherever they could be had. Fry himself was the last of the great pan-athletes. He held the English high jump record for twenty-one years, played soccer for England and in an FA Cup Final for Southampton, as well as being a first-rate scholar, writer, and later diplomat. All this was in addition to his achievements in cricket, where he had six years at the top of the first-class batting averages and a career average of over fifty. None the less, he was less esteemed by his contemporaries than other less prolific but more traditional batsmen. Gentleman or not, C.B. Fry was the first batsman to take a professional approach to the game, taking runs wherever they were offered, but never running risks in the interests of some concept of style. By the end of the Edwardian era he was opening the England innings with Jack Hobbs, and a new and more pragmatic age of cricket had begun.

C. B. Fry

The clouds of war were then poised to blot out the sunshine. But there were other clouds that had always hovered over sport and recreation. Behind the smooth surface of its polite play there had always lurked another sporting life that was largely hidden or glossed over. It was not merely the widespread unreconstructed play of the working classes, with its rough and ready bareknuckle fights in the back rooms of East End public houses, its Black Country dog-fighting, its pitch and toss gambling in any hidden corner, its Sunday morning whippet-racing on the London marshes. Even the noble game itself had its blemishes and its crowd problems. The University cricket matches of 1893 and 1896 were both controversial because Cambridge deliberately gave runs away so that Oxford would not take the then compulsory follow-on. In the latter match, the players were booed, jeered, and physically jostled by MCC members when they returned to the pavilion. Again, in the first test match against the Australians in 1905 there was a similar incident and with such examples from members it is hardly surprising that the paying customers also gave occasional vent to their frustrations, and to even more direct action, as when the crowd at the Middlesex v. Lancashire game in 1907 tore up the pitch in anger at an unexplained rain delay.

More insidious were the racist attitudes which permeated the upper reaches of the game. The highly gifted batsman, K.S. Ranjitsinjhe, only scraped his blue at Cambridge in his final year, in spite of his obvious worth, and, at a time when the home club still chose the England team, racial prejudice within the MCC kept him out of the Lords test. Fortunately, more liberal attitudes prevailed in Surrey and Lancashire, with happy results for England, and success for Ranji himself. Nor at the county level was it all prosperity and high achievement. Some county clubs were in deep trouble, such as Somerset, who cut down their fixtures in 1910, simply to save money, lost 15 of their games, won none, used nearly forty players, and gave their professional, Fred Hardy, no fewer than nine different opening partners.

It was this same Fred Hardy who, a few years later, was to commit suicide to avoid having to return to the horrors of the Western Front, yet another sporting death to add to the tragedies that tarnished this golden age. When Emily Davison threw herself under the hooves of the king's horse, Amner, in the 1913 Derby, it was an act that highlighted the tensions and frictions that were inherent in the social and sporting circumstance of the day. At least as significant was the reporting of the event. The *Daily Express* gave 1,500 words to its account of the race, dwelt on the half-hour delay while the stewards reached a decision over the result, but it made no mention at all of the suffragette's self-destruction.

The People's Game
Newspapers, and particularly those that saw themselves at the quality end of the market, did not necessarily reflect the interests of the people as a whole, whether in sport or other matters. *The Times*, for instance, in those pre-war years, gave only scant coverage to soccer, but over all the British Isles one or other of the football codes had come to provide the masses with their major sporting entertainment. The association game held sway in England and Scotland, rugby in Wales, and a mix in Ireland, with soccer dominating the Scots-biased north, and the handling game more common in the south. The Gaelic Athletic Association, too, in active sympathy with nationalist politics, was promoting

the Irish form of football. In soccer, the Irish Football Association actually ante-dated the Scottish FA by some twelve months, and while it was originally weighted towards Belfast and northern clubs, it soon included teams from Dublin and the rest of the country. These latter would eventually form the basis of the League of Ireland after partition. The religious and political divisions underlying the strife in Ireland were shared by Glasgow, whose two great professional clubs each had its solid affiliation, with Glasgow Celtic originally founded to raise funds for Catholic charities, and Rangers assertively Protestant in its management, its players, and its crowds.

The English Football League, in 1900, was still overwhelmingly the preserve of the North and the West Midlands. Originally established in 1889 to ensure a regular programme of attractive fixtures instead of uncertain friendly matches, it consisted of clubs with large populations on hand and a keenness to capture steady gates. Not until a second division was added to the league, and expanded a year later, was room found for a single southern club, and then it was Woolwich Arsenal, well-known for its recruitment of northern and Scottish players as workers. Other southern clubs grew through the same means, but the geographical bias in the Football League was slow to change. Southampton, from the Southern League, whose team was based originally on northern shipbuilders, might reach the FA Cup Final in both 1900 and 1902, but did not gain entrance to the Football League until the early 1920s, when there was further expansion. Immediately after the 1914-18 war, when the two divisions had 22 clubs each, southern representation was still limited to Arsenal and Chelsea in Division I and just five clubs in Division II. Two decades later, there were still only five teams from anywhere south of Birmingham in the premier league, and three of these were struggling near the bottom. The cup went to Portsmouth in 1939, but otherwise the last sixteen in the competition included only Chelsea and West Ham United from outside the game's original professional heartland.

The takeover of association football by the northern professionals was viewed with distaste by many of the game's first promoters. A notable product of the anti-professional mood was the creation of the Corinthians, a team of outstanding amateur players, who conspicuously eschewed all organised competition, but who proved a match for the cream of the professional sides during the first twenty years of their existence. Better nurture, bigger frames, early training, and greater energy and leisure can go a long way to explaining their superiority, though critics of the professional game would put it down to moral fibre, manliness, and uprightness of character. It was in this spirit that the whole amateur soccer world (and C.B. Fry's voice was one of the loudest) protested at the introduction of the penalty kick, on the grounds that no gentleman would ever deliberately foul. The same rejection of the professional ethos brought the amateurs to put up their own competition, and if the Football Association's first response (as always to something new) was to oppose, the Amateur Cup was sanctioned in time for the 1893/4 season. Any hope that it might help to restore southern soccer pride was soon quashed as it was won initially by such north-eastern teams as Bishop Auckland, Crook Town, and Blythe Spartans, who were to remain leading contenders through the half century of the cup's lifetime. Amateur internationals between the home countries and against European opposition followed in the early twentieth century.

The limited facilities that still exist on football league grounds

The moral rectitude of the amateur stance was, however, by no means unsullied. Leading amateurs would sometimes only play their games for a financial guarantee, or for a share of the gate money, and so would walk away from the match better off than their professional colleagues. This was not difficult, as the professional's maximum wage was set at £4 a week in 1900. This was only one of the constraints which kept the paid player firmly in his place, tied him to his club, and presented a constant invitation to corruption. George Parsonage was banned for life when he made the mistake of asking directly for £50, instead of the £10 maximum allowed, when he was being transferred from Fulham to Chesterfield. Such matters were to be conducted by winks and nods. Undercover payments were rife, and those few cases which surfaced - with Manchester City in 1905, and the long-running saga of Middlesbrough irregularities from then until 1911 - were only the tips of the iceberg. The absence of a maximum wage in Scotland meant that the richer clubs, Rangers, Celtic, and Hearts, could buy up the best talent, and the same applied to the Southern League until 1906, which explains its clubs' regular successes against league opposition in the early years of the century.

The fans cared little about such financial peccadilloes, nor about the fulminations of critics over the mercenary turn the game had taken, with teams often having little link through their players with their neighbourhood. This was no deterrent to the fans. If the players wore their colours, they were their men. Soccer continued to go from strength to strength even through the hardest depression years between the wars. Indeed, the local soccer club could often become almost the only symbol of hope for the unemployed and the short-time worker, the only regular prospect of greater glory in their drab and poverty-stricken world. Nor did it end with the match itself, as the local newspaper would have its special football edition, pink, buff, or green, on sale within an hour of the finish of the Saturday match, bringing queues flocking to the news-stands, avid for every detail of the team's doings.

Pitch invasions and crowd disorder were almost inevitable, given the passions that the game aroused. They were, however, usually related directly to events on the pitch or to deep-seated sectarian divisions, and were not comparable to the ritualistic conflicts of latter days, for which the football match has provided the occasion rather than the cause. There are many examples. Spectators in Belfast delayed the start of the international against Scotland in 1902, when the police lost control. A specifically religious battle flared up at half-time at a Belfast Celtic game against Linfield in 1912, ending with about a hundred injured laid out on the pitch. In Scotland, one Hampden Park cup final replay again resulted in a draw and the crowd rebelled at the prospect of yet another entrance charge. Again nearly a hundred spectators and police needed hospital treatment, planks and rails were smashed and set alight, and there was general chaos. Attacks on visiting teams were common, after any particularly tense game. In 1911, for instance, the Preston charabanc was pelted with every missile that came to hand as it left Hillsborough following a drawn game with Sheffield Wednesday, and the outside passengers of every tramcar that it overtook turned and spat in the faces of the Preston contingent.

Polished behaviour from football crowds was not encouraged by the spartan conditions of most grounds. There might be large investment in some stadia - Manchester United, Everton, and Blackburn, for instance, all spent over £30,000 on new stands in the first decade of the century, but for the most part the paying spectator had to endure the most rudimentary facilities, heavily dependent on corrugated iron sheeting for any shelter, and on beaten cinder underfoot. Toilet facilities, especially for women, were virtually non-existent, and communication with spectators was minimal, running at best to a man carrying a blackboard round the ground. Such aids to identification as the numbering of shirts, first introduced to the sporting public by the touring rugby team from New Zealand as early as 1905, was laughed to scorn by football's administrators, and only introduced into the game by Tottenham Hotspur and other forward-looking clubs some thirty years later. The one really innovative path was beaten by Arsenal, under the forceful and imaginative managership of Herbert Chapman in the 1930s. Not only did he create a team strong enough to break the long stranglehold of the midland and northern clubs and take the championship from them on five occasions, he also saw a new stadium arise, concrete rather than iron sheeting, and a model for its times. As a final triumph, Chapman even persuaded the London Passenger Transport Board, at great expense, to change the name of the local tube station to that of the football club - 'Arsenal'.

In spite of the poverty of its facilities in the British Isles, football continued to flourish both there and beyond. The limited number of wealthy Scottish clubs meant that Scots professionals continued to be drawn in large numbers to the better-off English teams, but the national side was well able to hold its own. Irish soccer was more unsettled, especially after partition and a long wrangle, finally settled by the International Football Federation, over which part of the island was entitled to call itself the 'Irish FA'. They became the Northern Ireland FA and the Republic of Ireland FA, a solution which seemed obvious enough to all but those closely involved. Both, too, found continued competition from the intensely nationalist Gaelic form, a legitimate focus still for political passions, its Belfast headquarters bearing the challenging name of Casement Park.

In the early nineteenth century soccer spread rapidly over Europe. The German FA was established in 1900, the Swedish in 1904, and the French in 1919. British football, though, remained cocooned in its own complacent self-regard, playing its home international matches, and deriving its patriotic satisfactions from them. European football was not entirely ignored, but it was scarcely taken seriously. When the world body for the game, FIFA, was formed in 1904, the Football Association regarded it as an upstart organisation, muscling in on a British game. The home associations remained aloof. They joined later, with the English, Welsh, Scottish and Irish all being allowed individual representation (that they still are is a constant irritant to most FIFA members), but they were seldom in much sympathy, and withdrew in the 1920s over the definition of amateurism. The conviction that British football was bound to be the best in the world was not to be disturbed by such occasional vagaries as the defeat of England by Spain in 1929, or by such new-fangled trumperies as a World Cup. The revelation of where the British had really come to stand in their national game would only come after the long break of the Second World War.

By contrast, rugby football had followed cricket into whole-hearted international play, even though both games were largely confined within the Anglo-Saxon and colonial worlds. There had been a rugby tour of Australia as early as 1880, organised by the old Nottinghamshire cricket professionals, Shaw and Shrewsbury, building on their previous experience of taking cricket teams. At this stage, the enterprise was reminiscent of the tours at home by the earlier professional cricketers, the players acting as much as entertainers and missionaries for the game as serious competitors. More genuine rivalry soon took the place of one-sided exhibitions, and by 1914 tours had taken place, home and away, against Australia, New Zealand, and South Africa. Nearer home, France was included in the international championship from the 1905/6 season, though here again relationships with Europe were uneasy. There were no games against the French for much of the 1930s, when rugby was in a more than usually dubious state of amateurism and other matters.

The fortunes of the home countries fluctuated. The rapid rise of Welsh rugby coincided with the loss of Yorkshire and Lancashire players, the backbone of the English team, to the new Northern League, and this left the Welsh supreme in the first decade of the century. The English revival, glimpsed at after 1910, only came after the First World War, when Adrian Stoop managed to achieve something similar to Herbert Chapman in the other code, reviving Harlequins, and through Harlequins and the development of Twickenham set English rugby on its feet once more. Even in the south of England, though, Rugby Union was not the people's game. Only in a few areas, such as Cornwall and other parts of the far West Country did it have the following elsewhere accorded to soccer or, in the North, also to Rugby League. In Scotland, too, it was only in the borders that the union game had priority, significantly another region where professional soccer had made virtually no headway. Only in Wales was it securely the sport that came first with the mass of the population.

Female running match, from the early nineteenth century (*Sporting Magazine*)

The fact that, between them, the various football styles had covered the kingdom was significant of itself. What is more, it was symptomatic of a popular involvement in organised sport that was rapidly expanding, well beyond a single game, and increasingly spreading across both sexes and all social groups.

More Play: More Players

When Gertrude Ederle swam the English Channel in 1926 she was not only the first woman to do so, but also knocked two hours off the best male time for the swim. It was an important moment in the history of women's sport. Channel swimming had no potential at all as a mass participation sport, but it did arouse mass interest. Even so, the challenge was so commonly taken up (six more women made the trip within months) that it became according to one contemporary, 'all a bit of a bore.' The success of these women swimmers nevertheless had its impact, encouraging others to share in the considerable growth of the skill. The trip to the seaside and the annual holiday there did something to counteract the comparatively slow provision of new public facilities after the burst of Victorian building. Swimming was open to all, from schooldays upwards now that it had become a common addition to the curriculum.

At the other, exclusive, end of the sporting market, polo, yachting, motor-racing and skiing all flourished. With the winter sports, and with motor-racing in the inter-war years, the exclusivity was one of wealth, not of gender. Women took their full part in both. Winter sports expanded so rapidly that sleeping cars to the Alps were booked up many months in advance of the season, in spite of the financial calls for expensive equipment and hotels and the availability of ample leisure. It was the cavalier age of motor sports, still dominated by wealthy individuals as well as motor manufacturers and works teams. The dramatic high banks of the Brooklands track roared and throbbed to the powerful Bentleys, Maseratis, and Alfa-Romeos as they swept round the circuit. Motor-cycling found itself an available track on the public roads of the Isle of Man, where the tourist trophy races became a great annual gathering. Both sports dated from the first decade of the century, but for both, the inter-war years were their high point. So it was, too, for feats in the air, where there were endless 'firsts' to be accomplished, and fastest times to be set. There was an insatiable public interest in the pioneering flying heroes, particularly if they were women such as Amy Johnson or Amelia Earhart. Locally, the interest was catered for by small-scale air races, and aerobatic and parachuting displays, often by touring entertainers who took their machinery from the present day but their style from the past.

While some sports might have to remain elitist on the grounds of cost and time, others such as field hockey, rowing and, outside Scotland, golf *chose* to do so, though sometimes with some excuse. Hockey, for instance, had little spectator appeal and could not look to gate money for funds. Its clubs had little

Mrs Thornton - the exclusion of women from active sport was a Victorian phenomenon. Mrs Thornton, wife of a noted Yorkshire sportsman, rode a match against Mr Flint on York racecourse, allegedly before 100,000 spectators, in August 1804. The fact that she lost was put down simply to the fact that she had to ride side-saddle *(Sporting Magazine)*.

incentive to expand. Rowing, similarly, could provide exciting spectacles, but its crowds were impossible to exploit - the many thousands who watched the Boat Race annually from the banks of the Thames (and more did so than ever before) made no contribution at all to the race beyond their somewhat inexplicable enthusiasm. Golf was still not a spectator sport to any extent, and the pressure for more facilities continued to be met much more through private, usually socially selective, clubs than through public courses. Only a minority of local government authorities made any widely available provision by building municipal courses. There was, indeed, a reinforcing rather than a weakening of class discrimination in many sports, and among the manifestations of this was the steady switch by public schools from soccer to rugby as the winter game, the latter being considered more gentlemanly. Interestingly, a similar process took place after the 1939-45 war within the state educational system, with quite a number of northern secondary schools moving from rugby league to union as a sign of social and educational ambition.

Ladies made their way in golf and tennis, among the established sports. Championship play for lady golfers began at the end of the nineteenth century and the lady golfer was accepted, so long as she kept in her place, frequently quarantined to particular areas of the clubhouse, and denied access to the course at the times most popular with the male members. Many golf clubs defied convention and history by opening on Sundays, but where they did it was often for male members only. Doubtless they wished to protect their ladies from the possibility of sinning against the commandments. The Ladies' Golf Union tended to be conservative and deferential, demanding, for instance, skirts of a decorous length, and expressing its regret when a competitor in the 1933 championship appeared in slacks and sweater. It took a war to make such attire respectable.

Long skirts and heavy dresses had been even more of an encumbrance to women players on the tennis courts, and they had made their bid for comparative freedom much earlier. The success of Suzanne Lenglen, the dynamic French player, set both new styles of play and new styles of dress - light, shorter skirts which gave a much greater freedom of movement. Lenglen herself, with half a dozen years of virtually unchallenged success behind her, eventually antago-nised the tennis public by turning up late for a match in 1926, one that Queen Mary had gone to Wimbledon particularly to watch. She then set another noteworthy precedent by signing up as a professional in the United States and setting up a tennis school in Paris. At championship levels tennis had certainly established itself as a spectator sport, but it remained a determinedly amateur game firmly rooted in the middle classes. Tennis clubs remained the basis of the game in the country and were usually at least as socially exclusive as their golfing counterparts. Public courts did begin to be provided more commonly by local councils, but these were invariably with tarmac surfaces.

Women's athletics also began its slow and still incomplete march towards parity with the male sport. The Amateur Athletic Association proved reluctant to have male and female events organised together, and the Women's AAA was formed in 1922. The international development of women's competition was also hesitant - they were only introduced into the Olympics at Amsterdam in 1928, when the British refused to participate as the women were allocated five events only. The progress of women's hockey and cricket was likewise steady

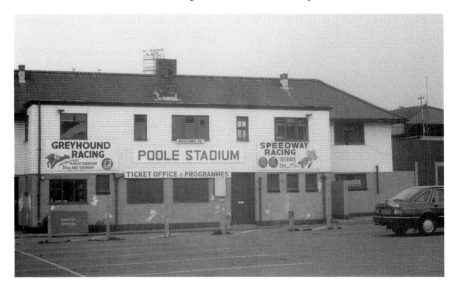

Poole Stadium. A rare example of a multi-sport facility, housing greyhound and speedway racing, as well as non-league soccer

if subdued during these inter-war years, prompted mainly by the involvement of girls' independent schools, following the athletic ethos of their male counterparts, and upholding the same social tone.

On the wider sporting scene, horse-racing remained poised somewhat uneasily between the aristocratic control of the Jockey Club and the raffish company of the race gangs which plagued many courses in the immediate post-war years. After the formation of the Bookmakers' Protection Association in 1921, disorder became much less frequent. The sport became even better regulated in the 1930s following the establishment of the Racecourse Betting Control Board and the advent of the totalisator, with its assurance of fair returns from wagers. There were, though, two new rivals for the punters' shillings, in the football pools and greyhound-racing. The growth of the pools was phenomenal. The £20 million being staked in 1934/5 was doubled within two years, helped immeasurably by the pools' avoidance of the Gaming Acts, the judges having decided, in their wisdom, that skill was involved in selecting likely results. Irish Hospital Sweepstake tickets were also widely available and traded, in spite of their illegality.

Greyhound-racing, too, leapt into sudden popularity in the early 1930s. The decisive step came with the introduction of the electric hare, first installed at Belle Vue, Manchester, in July 1929, and attracting a 27,000 crowd to the first meeting at which it was used. Within a year there were no less than sixty companies mounting greyhound-racing. It was a sport which lent itself to rapid expansion. The competitors themselves could be bred and trained quickly and the capital investment needed to set up meetings was relatively modest. Almost any football ground could squeeze in a track around its periphery, and a great many did so, though few now remain in such dual use. If a ground happened not to be available, a rudimentary stadium could be knocked up rapidly, without planning or safety problems, and the floodlighting (for what was essentially an evening sport) was much less demanding than that needed for football. Like the football pools, 'the dogs' were particularly attractive to the man whose betting was small-scale, but the frequency of meetings - often five a week - meant that the temptations were persistent and 'going to the dogs' quickly acquired a meaning not confined to the sport that inspired it.

Another new competitive venture which could sometimes share football grounds, though much less comfortably, was speedway racing. Its space demands made it difficult to accommodate successfully in most existing stadia, but it carved its own niche in the burgeoning sporting market of the 1930s. In a period of almost constant expansion of popular sport, it is worth noting that some of the older competitors for leisure time fared less well. Roller-skating went through one of its periods of slump, while ice-skating had only scattered indoor provision. What did thrive were other and smaller-scale indoor games, such as billiards and darts. Professional championship billiards reduced itself to eventual farce when the highly skilled discovered how to produce interminable breaks from repeated cannons of the balls lodged tightly against the cushion. The change of rules to prevent this hardly brought back the game to its former public pre-eminence, but the working man's billiards lost none of its popularity, in spite of the rather dubious reputation of some public billiard halls as the jaunts of cigarette-smoking layabouts. It was a remarkable class transition in a game which had, a generation before, been the after-dinner pursuit of the country house. Darts, on the other hand, managed to make what proved to be a temporary move upmarket. Previously a game of the working man and the public bar, it suddenly took off and extended its appeal when the king and queen were pictured playing, and the dart board became an essential piece of sporting equipment in every home.

Royal approval or not, there were the usual doubts about the direction being taken by popular sport. The international failures of British players became increasingly common. There was only one British women's singles winner at Wimbledon in the inter-war years, and competition, particularly from across the Atlantic, was proving increasingly difficult to cope with in a whole variety of sports from golf to swimming. These set-backs might be shrugged off, but there was still suspicion that the sporting growth of the times was too heavily weighted towards gambling activities and towards recreation which made only limited physical demands, often in environments not conducive to good health. One reason for this was simply lack of facilities. The desire for active play had far outstripped the provision made for it - in 1929 the London County Council had some 350 football pitches and over a thousand clubs wanting to use them. In spite of the founding of the National Playing Fields Association in 1926 and the Central Council for Recreative Physical Education in 1935, the most successful of the 'healthy' recreations were those that needed no specialist facilities but made use of the countryside. Canoeing, climbing, pot-holing, and, above all, walking and rambling, all grew in popularity. 'Hiking' characterised the government inspired 'Keep Fit' movement of the thirties. It was a distant relation of the 'Strength through Joy' concept which was helping to further the fascist cause in Germany, which in turn was about to bring the strange and half-real world of the twenties and thirties most savagely to its conclusion.

The Living Past VI

The living past comes ever closer to being the living present. The inter-war years still survive in the memories of a great many older people, and it is important that they should not be lost. There are occasional opportunities to reach back even further, to childhood days before 1914, and memories handed on to older people by their own parents can take the record back even further into the last century. It is important that these are recorded, wherever possible, and important that these older people should particularly try to give a picture of those elements in sport which tended to escape contemporary commentators. Useful leading questions could include these: what sports or games were you involved in? Did you watch or play? How often, and when? What did it cost? What sort of people went to watch or play? Did you go as a group, if so how was the group made up? How did you travel? Would you travel far for sport? Was the behaviour of players and spectators different from what it is today? Did you do any training, or have any coaching? Do you know anything about how your professional team trained?

Frequently the responses will dwell on individual matches, and these, too, can be enlightening, but check them against the published records. Memory can filter and reshape the facts over the years!

The early sporting memories of older ladies are particularly interesting to recall. Those with a secondary or grammar school education are likely to have enjoyed playing opportunities from childhood, but others may have come to sport later in life - or never developed any sporting interests at all, until television thrust it upon them. Many learned to swim after childhood during the inter-war years and it is interesting to discover how they did so, given the patchy nature of the facilities. Old photographs of sporting events, apart from their intrinsic value, can often trigger memories and give rise to helpful comments.

Both the written record and the physical reminders of these years are, of course, plentiful. Some country-house cricket grounds, for instance, are still in use - Thoresby Park in Nottinghamshire and Stalbridge in Dorset are just two of many - and they usually retain an attraction that makes them worth visiting. Many country houses, too, must still have records and probably scorebooks, dating from the days when they mounted their own cricket parties. Writing on cricket abounds, with Neville Cardus the most prominent, though his romantic creativity has to be taken into account. It was perhaps best summed up by Emmot Robinson's retort to him; 'Ah reckon, Mr Cardus, tha's invented me!' And although county cricket is now well written up, much still remains to be done in local cricket history. Reports of all local sports clubs, including their annual general meetings and dinners, were usually much more fully reported in the town newspaper than they would be later, and even if actual records of the clubs have not survived these accounts can often reveal a great deal about the club's activities, its social make-up, the motives of the members, any criticisms they might have to meet (golf and cycling often faced sabbatarian attacks) and how they responded to them.

Most football league clubs now have their own histories in some shape or form, as, indeed, do many clubs of humbler status. While many such accounts are properly fired by club enthusiasm and loyalty, and vary in their historical insights, virtually all have some usefulness. What are less available are accounts of local competitions, leagues and cups, and of clubs which have since disappeared - the flourishing 'early closing' leagues and clubs that existed for some fifty years before the 1939 war come particularly to mind, and the early history of the Sunday leagues. Similarly, the history and photographic record of early football grounds is often deficient and may present an opportunity for local research.

Less tangible reminders of the fairly recent past are still to be found in some sport literature. The old establishment athleticism continues to assert itself from time to time. Even in the 1960s one writer was describing league cricket as an alternative form 'to the friendly club atmosphere so prevalent in the south,' with the club cricketer playing 'for his own enjoyment' and his league counterpart 'always conscious of the crowd element,' a distinction incomprehensible to anyone who has played both. Even the admirable BBC Test Match Special, with its ball-by-ball commentaries, often comes near to being a parody of itself, and redounds with old attitudes of fairness and good form, claiming, for instance, that the crowd would like to see a big innings from a famous visitor, when most British spectators would love to see him bowled neck and crop, first ball. Current controversies over cash rewards for Rugby Union players, and over the amateurism or otherwise of the Olympic Games are more than likely to reawaken similar echoes of historical attitudes.

Suggestions for further reading become increasingly difficult as the story comes nearer to our own day, and not from the absence of useful sources but from their abundance. We have moved, for instance, into the era of the sportsman's biography (and later the sportswoman's), notably marked by W.G. Grace, *Cricketing Reminiscences and Personal Recollections* (London, 1899, reprinted 1980). Biographies, too, are often rewarding, as with Peter Wynne-Thomas, *'Give me Arthur' A Biography of Arthur Shrewsbury* (London, 1985) which makes excellent use of the cricketer's previously unpublished correspondence, particularly on the financing of Australian tours. The histories of individual sports already mentioned have their continuing relevance, and a new dimension on spectator sport is found in Wray Vamplew, *Pay up and play the game: Professional Sport in Britain 1875-1914* (Cambridge, 1988), concerned with the developing economics of play. Another view of sport is found in Simon Inglis, *Soccer in the Dock: A History of British Football Scandals 1900-1963* (London, 1985). There are, finally, a number of books which give the feel of past decades, and help to put sport into its wider social context - among these are Robert Graves and Alan Hodge, *The Long Week-End: A Social History of Great Britain 1918-1939* (London, 1940) and Harry Hopkins, *The New Look: A Social History of the Forties and Fifties in Britain* (London, 1969).

Examples of sponsorship

7

Britain in a Sporting World

The first sporting revolution, in the late nineteenth century, made sport regular, nationally organised, commercially aware, and a matter of wide public interest. The second sporting revolution of the later twentieth century has made it international, freed it from restrictions of clock and season, and made it universally accessible. While the British contribution to that first revolution was central, the role of Britain in the second has been increasingly marginal. Even so, it is voluminously recorded in an endless flood of sports writing - every sport has its shelves of books and its growing collection of videotapes, and every sportsman of the slightest note finds it obligatory to have an autobiography produced in his or her name. Reflective comment on the recent past is inevitably much rarer, without the benefit of any lengthy historical perspective. The ages nearest to our own are always the hardest to evaluate. The judgements of history, made with the opportunity to digest the facts and see their consequences, seldom matches the convictions of those involved at the time. All that is possible in an overall survey of the whole story of British sport is to pick up some recent themes in the hope that history will find them equally significant in retrospect.

Modern sport has many important aspects. Among these are its politics, its money, and its international dimension. Pleas to 'keep politics out of sport' are among the emptier slogans of our age. In the simplest terms, if politics is the art of living together, and if play is part of that living, the two are inextricably interlinked. At the practical level, no less an authority than the former chairman of the International Olympic Committee, Lord Killanin, has unequivocally asserted that 'politics are "in" sport and have always been.' Money has been a major interest in sport for centuries, but its role has changed decisively in the last half century. It now means much more than counting the shillings in the gate money. Sport has become very big business. The sums involved now run into millions - in television rights, in sponsorships, and in the rewards available to the top managers, promoters and performers. By 1990 an insurance company would pay £5 million to sponsor cricket test matches, a darts player could win over £100,000 for throwing nine arrows into the right spaces on the board, and a thirty second advertisement during the screening of the American Superbowl cost $600,000, and the figures have continued to rise. The Amateur Athletic Association continues to receive four times as much income from television fees as from admission charges and this in turn is dwarfed by the sums injected into the Premiere League football clubs by satellite television in exchange for live broadcast rights. It covers the globe, and, through television, it has become internationally and instantly available.

Politics, Wars, and Play

There must be scarcely a country whose sport history does not demonstrate some interaction with its politics. This not only applies where sport has been deliberately used to promote political attitudes as in Nazi Germany but also, and more justifiably, where countries have found sporting success to be one of the cheapest means to achieve world recognition. More people around the world heard of Cameroon from their 1990 successes in the soccer World Cup than had done so during the whole of the country's previous existence. Even in Britain, where the government disposition has always been to keep sport at arm's length and to intervene only out of necessity, the interaction between sport and politics has been persistent, from the medieval royal commands for archery practice onwards. In the nineteenth century, all the various worries over the state of the nation brought up issues of public health and recreational provision of parks and public open spaces, and of swimming baths, and produced some embryonic physical education even in the state schools.

In the later twentieth century, almost every government action will impinge on sport in some way or other. Changes in employment law and most fiscal steps will affect professional sport, while actions on public order and the administration of justice will affect sporting crowds. Political issues, in peace and war alike, have their implications for the country's play, expanding opportunities at some times, restricting them at others.

At its most radical, in wartime, government interest has been able to push aside the strongest taboos, such as those restricting Sunday play. Sunday militia drilling came in during the Napoleonic Wars and then Sunday rifle competitions during the struggle with the Boers. During the two world wars the Sabbath restraints also collapsed, with much games playing allowed to members of the services and war workers, while hundreds of thousands overseas experienced a games-playing continental Sunday, and found it one of the least corrupting of their wartime experiences. The lasting consequences after 1918 were limited to a growth of Sunday cricket (which many clubs sought to disguise by giving different names to their Sunday teams), a little more Sunday rowing, and the usual Sunday play in golf and tennis clubs.

Organised sport in both wars was reduced to a minimum. The continuation of football and horse-racing after 1914 brought much criticism. In spite of the numerous players who enlisted in the sportsmen's battalions, soccer had the reputation of being 'unpatriotic' as the game did continue, in regional leagues. Horse-racing continued, on a reduced scale - there were even complaints to the press about the shortage of taxis at Gatwick Races in 1916! Government did impose restrictions. By 1918 there were some 80 days of racing still allowed, half of them at Newmarket, the rest allocated to areas of concentrated war production.

The First World War saw the last flowering of the athletic tradition nurtured so fondly by the late Victorians and the Edwardians. It prompted thousands of young sportsmen to volunteer to serve king and country, and could provoke acts of tragically incongruous gallantry. Edgar Mobbs, Northampton and England rugby player, raised his own company of his county's sportsmen, and led an attack out of the trenches by kicking up a rugby ball high into No Man's Land and chasing forward to follow up. He is still celebrated in the annual memorial match played between East Midlands and the Barbarians. It was not just a brave man who died, it was also an ideal. The delusion of athleticism was that sport and life are identical, and it was a delusion which could not survive the horrors of twentieth-century war.

The 1939-45 conflict produced much the same wartime sporting pattern. Football continued, but in regional leagues, with scratch, unpredictable teams, and to small and diminishing crowds. Among the amateur clubs, many moved to Sunday play, as the only day commonly free from work. The change became so ingrained that there were over 3,000 clubs playing on the Sabbath by the early 1950s, in spite of their blatant contravention of the FA's rule 25. Eventually, the ban was quietly rescinded. County cricket disappeared with the outbreak of war, which had been conveniently delayed until the effective end of the season. Club and league cricket, however, continued, often enlivened by the presence of first-class or even test match players. Later in the war, with beaches and seaside resorts inaccessible, the organised 'Holidays at Home' weeks often had a string of cricket matches as a central feature. In the West Midlands, for instance, in 1942, matches being advertised included a two-day game between Birmingham and District League XI and London Civil Defence (which would include Compton) and a Coventry and District League XI ('largely county players') and a London Counties XI. Play in these wartime games in high summer was often scheduled to go on until 8.00 pm, a foretaste of what was to come in the one-day cup contests of post-war years.

By the end of the war large crowds were going to two-day matches - Saturday and Sunday - between services teams of the highest quality, often including commonwealth test stars as well as home players. Rugby, too, had its 'Services Internationals' and in these and other forces' matches Union and League players shared the same field, though the play was under Union rules, giving each a unique opportunity to get the feel of the other's mode of playing the game. However, in spite of these highlights, sport at the highest levels remained severely restricted, not least because of the requisitioning of so many sporting facilities. By the end of the conflict, only half a dozen racecourses remained in use, and their meetings were confined to locally trained horses. Many sporting venues had been put to more urgent uses. Pelham Warner, as MCC secretary, might successfully defend Lords, claiming its symbolic importance for the nation's morale, but Highbury was taken over for Civil Defence, Twickenham was dug up to provide allotments, and the Oval became a prisoner-of-war camp.

Some longer-term changes were given their impetus by the war. Many professional sportsmen, especially cricketers, were commissioned, and the line between the amateur and the paid player became more blurred. It still took more than a decade of peace for the barriers to fall in cricket and tennis, and only in the 1990s were they beginning to crumble in rugby, but the social structure and the sporting economics which they implied could only tenuously survive in the later twentieth century. Other forms of discrimination remained though, to present future problems, sporting and political.

Racial prejudice was to raise a number of different issues. Colour bars had not previously played much part in British sports - particularly not in prizefighting where a black American, Tom Molyneux, had fought Tom Cribb for the Championship as early as 1810, and many other black fighters were to make some mark or other in the prize ring. By and large, non-white performers in any sport just had to put up with the constraints imposed on all working-class players, though in their case these were often writ large. In the first half of this century, the actions of the sporting establishment tended to reflect attitudes even more damaging than popular racial prejudice, in, for instance, its reluctance to accept Ranjitsinjhi. Even more remarkable was the continuing readiness of rugby and cricket administrators to bow to pressure from South Africa. This began even before the apartheid years, and was not just applied to tours there - Duleepsinjhi found himself dropped from the English team when the South Africans were touring Britain in the late 1920s. When the break did finally come it was as a result of the D'Oliveira case in 1968, and was only after the selectors had sought every means of excluding the 'coloured' South African from the original team, in an attempt to avoid the crisis his inclusion would precipitate. They reluctantly included him only because there was no alternative to his selection when the party's all-rounder stepped down because of injury. The tour was cancelled, marking the end of official fixtures between the two countries. Of all the governing bodies of the major team sports, Rugby Union, held out the longest in support of links with South Africa, in the teeth of world opinion.

The withdrawal of Olympic recognition of South Africa in 1971 was just one sporting contribution to the international efforts to end apartheid. There can be little doubt that these exclusions caused considerable frustration in a sport-loving and previously successful country and that they were at least a factor in the movement towards reform in the early 1990s. Originally, they had raised the usual protests against allowing politics to interfere with sport, which usually means, in fact, an objection to any politics which the administrators dislike. The objectors can themselves be ready to use sport for other political ends - witness, for instance, the blatant nationalism of the Los Angeles Olympics. England's footballers were prevailed upon to give the Nazi salute before their match in Berlin in 1938, a gesture perhaps, but such gestures have their significance, whether they are the outstretched arms and open palms or the clenched fists of Black Power. And cancelled fixtures are always better than bombs and bloodshed. The continuing sensitivity of sport to political issues was well illustrated in March 1992, when a 'No' vote in the Anti-Apartheid referendum would almost certainly have led to the withdrawal of the South African team from cricket's World Cup semi-final.

British governments only began to make a formal long-term commitment to sport under Harold Wilson. Dennis Howell, a former first-class football referee, had for some ten years had sport among his responsibilities as an under-secretary tucked away in the backwaters of the Ministry of Education. Then, in 1974, as Minister of State for the Environment he became effectively the first fully-fledged Minister for Sport. At first the minister's role was positive and promotional, but under the Thatcher administration in the 1980s it took another turn. Politicians became preoccupied by the disorderly and sometimes violent behaviour of football crowds while, at the same time, they were reluctant to look anywhere outside the game itself for the root causes. The Heysel Stadium disaster, when 37 died, in a panic flight from fighting Liverpool and Juventus fans, was the final straw for a Prime Minister who had tired of having to apologise to European colleagues. The even more tragic Hillsborough disaster of 1989 confirmed what many thought at the time - that the real danger was from inadequate stewarding and supervision in old and unsafe grounds, more than from rioting supporters. The Football Spectators Bill was pushed relentlessly through, in spite of the opposition of virtually every football interest, but in the end the worst of its bite was moderated. The determination to control football, even at the expense of its very existence, gradually softened to more rational levels, and the scale of the problem of hooliganism slowly lessened.

There was a softening of attitudes under the premiership of John Major who did have a genuine love of cricket if little else to give sport. Now its politics have many dimensions. A reputation made in sport can be a ticket to a political career, as with Christopher Chattaway and Sebastian Coe. International sporting organisations readily take on overtones from national politics, echoing its alliances and its antagonisms. Success or failure of its sportsmen on the world stage even influences a people's attitude towards its government. Politics could, indeed, hardly be more integral to sport than it already is.

The Money and the Media

Over the years many heads have shaken at the 'corruption' of sport by cash. 'It is not good that a game should be a matter of money. Evil passions are excited,' and 'as soon as any sport has become so popular that money is to be made out of it, it may be prophesied with certainty that abuses will arise' - just two voices from over a century ago. Most contemporary financial involvement in sport today has been there from the start, at least through the whole history of sport as an organised activity. Some of it has been kept under firm control, such as the earnings of many professional players until quite recent times. Other financial elements have varied from time to time in significance. Gambling, for instance, the basis of much early competitive play, was supposedly limited to the responsible classes after the mid-Victorian legislation banned street and public house betting. It began to achieve a wider degree of acceptability with the Totalisator on the racecourse and the football pools, which managed to achieve an image more akin to that of a church raffle than of the devil. Gambling's rehabilitation was virtually complete when government itself produced its 'Premium Bonds' in 1956, and made totally acceptable by the introduction of the National Lottery in the 1990s, greeted with delight by the Arts Council and the Sports Council alike.

Within the individual sports, the barriers against betting fell one by one. After a fifty-year struggle to exclude gambling in the last century, Lords finally allowed the bookmakers in again, and BBC commentators were soon even willing to publicise the odds. When these were long against England winning the Headingly Test Match in 1981, two Australian players bet against their own side, to their considerable profit, and without incurring any serious consequences, though the administrators of some other sports would have been less lenient. Some five years earlier even Wimbledon had opened its doors to the bookmakers, and now the final constraint on sporting wagers has been removed by ending the statutory closing of betting shops on the Sabbath in 1994.

While the old concept of playing for stake money has largely disappeared, it still plays some part, particularly on the turf. Finance has, in fact, sometimes

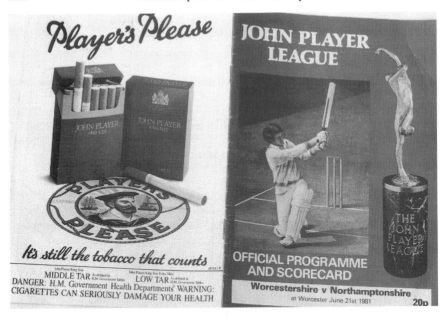

Sports Sponsorship. Cigarette manufacturers have found in county cricket advertising outlets which they would otherwise have no access to.

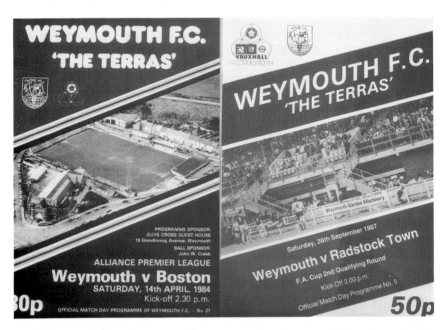

At the humbler levels of professional sport every scrap of sponsorship has its worth. Here, apart from the motor manufacturer's support of the whole competition, the programme itself and the ball for the match have their local sponsors.

been a means through which the Jockey Club has exercised its control, insisting on 'added money' for meetings, and this has come to play an ever-larger part in the sport's rewards to its winners. Two-thirds of the prize money still came from owners' fees at the turn of the century but, as a proportion, it has decreased steadily ever since. Corporate sponsorship has largely taken over in racing, as it has in many other sports, but personal sponsorship, which originally got many sports off the ground, continued for much longer than is often supposed, and still has lingering importance in some quarters. The benevolence of nineteenth-century sponsors has tended to be ignored because their style of financing seemed to belong to the more primitive stages of organised sport, yet personal support from local magnates could still initiate a race meeting (as the Duke of Portland did, by laying out the racecourse at Mansfield) just as the withdrawal of backing could mean its disappearance. It has been shown that Victorian patronage in central Scotland gave important impetus to a variety of sports including racing, bowls and curling, and well into the present century a county cricket club like Derbyshire would look to its patron, the Duke of Devonshire, to balance the books at the end of the season. Even personally involved sponsorship of the old type is not completely dead, nor have its original motives much altered - witness the vast expenditure of Alan Bond to take the America's Cup to Australia.

Most later twentieth-century sponsorship, though, tends to have more to do with profits than sentiment. Good pickings are to be had. Cigarette manufacturers have used sponsored events to bring their names before viewers through though this opportunity is likely to go the way of the existing ban on formally advertising their products on the screen. Cornhill Insurance found that public awareness rose dramatically as a result of their sponsorship of test matches, giving much cheaper results than could have been expected from direct advertising. But this commercial by-product of sport is far from new. Even before the end of the eighteenth century, the owners of London's pleasure gardens were giving annual prizes for yacht and sculling races, and by the mid-nineteenth century such sponsorship was commonplace. A glance at a single year's racing, in 1849, shows support from businessmen form all quarters (e.g., the Manchester Tradesmen's Cup of £300), from innkeepers in particular (at numerous meetings), and also from the railway company serving the town. What is new in the later twentieth century is the growing size of the sponsor's contribution, inflated enormously because its impact is no longer local, nor, frequently, merely national. A company name and logo may well flash repeatedly across the screens of the whole sporting world.

Locally, too commercial sponsorship has risen dramatically. Hospitality suites have sprouted all over the sporting scene and a company might pay up to £20,000 annually for one at a Premiere league football ground. This has even resulted in the reshaping of some sports such as cricket which actually ends its County Championship matches on Saturdays when the commercial sponsors know there is little prospect of attracting clients. It is a move which puts the paying spectator, looking for the assurance of a full day's play, firmly in his minority place. This sponsorship, members subscriptions, and a share in test match profits are what keep county clubs in being, not what is collected at the turnstiles. The spectator today is first and foremost the television viewer and the financial success of sport will be decided by how effectively it sells its product to him - and, often more especially - to her.

Increasingly too the major football clubs have converted themselves into limited companies, running the risk that considerations other than the sporting have major influences on the team.

Players themselves were slow to experience the benefit of the increasing amounts of money in sport. Jockeys were the first to benefit with some degree of regularity (as against the occasional windfall to one of the old pugilists, from a big win), with the best of the professional riders making £5,000 a year by the end of the nineteenth century, while footballers were earning little more than £200. Both they and the cricketers were kept on a tight financial rein until the second half of the nineteenth century. The early 1960s saw the abolition of the maximum wage in soccer and both soccer players and cricketers began to win some freedom of contract, loosening their dependence on their clubs. The old autocracy of football's management, however, remains reluctant to give any significant recognition to the claims of either organised spectators or unionised players. The move to a Premier League in 1992, which originally claimed to be a move towards reducing league fixtures for the top clubs, now appears to have been no more than a financial gambit, but eventually a highly successful one from which the top players take a full share of the gains. Apart from their negotiating of individual pay they are now free, once our of contract, to negotiate anywhere in the European Union on their own terms. As to the cricketers, their long-term financial security still usually depends on that reward for long service, the benefit. These are now much more systematically organised, covering a year or more of organised fund-raising events, with the benefit match itself playing a very minor role. It could often produce over £100,000. But this perpetuates a damaging system which keeps moderate players in the game longer than is good for it and limits the chances of up and coming youngsters.

The highest rewards come in the individual sports, such as motor-racing, tennis, golf, and snooker. The excessive riches, though, are only there for the best, and the stars, like sport itself, find themselves making even more from sponsorship and advertising contracts than from actual performance. The profits, are now invariably shared with that new protagonist of the later twentieth century, the players' agents.

The money has seldom, however, gone consistently into improving facilities. If British sporting salaries have become international, most of the facilities have remained parochial and poverty-stricken. Even the soccer ground improvements of the 1980s and those being planned and achieved for the millennium and beyond suffer from a double handicap, in the jealous isolation of individual clubs and the lack of public funding. No football stadium in Britain can hope to rival San Ciro in Milan until at least two great clubs agree to use the same venue and some municipal finance makes the venture possible. Still less will there be a Houston Astrodome, housing professional and college football, athletics, basketball and baseball, nor a Toronto Skydome, with its retractable roof, until there is an unprecedented coming-together of sporting organisations powerful enough to convince developers that there is a future in the vast investment needed. The lack of comfort in virtually all sporting venues (emphasised by the contrasting luxury of exclusive private boxes) continues to influence the make-up of British crowds and leaves the nation still with a massive task in promoting family spectating in most of its major sports through the improved facilities at the best grounds are helping to take football away from its former male working class base.

There remains though a generation of sports followers who have to be

The once rickety condition of Dorchester F.C., a senior non-league club.

The imaginative new facilities at Dorchester F.C.

The new facilities at Weymouth F.C.

Sport and television have now become inseparable and inter-dependent, and their symbiotic relationship is becoming increasingly apparent. Originally, sports administrators, seeing their live audiences shrink, were often antagonistic towards the new medium. The football leadership was particularly adamant, not only against allowing live soccer on the screens, but even reluctant and limiting over televised highlights of games. Eventually they realised that they needed television, for the wider interest that it maintained, more than television needed football, with so much other rival sport on offer. Cricket, for instance had accepted the lifeline of the small screen much earlier. A Sunday afternoon limited-over competition was specifically designed for the schedules of the newly arrived BBC second channel, one of the means by which the game rescued itself after the desperate fall in its live audience in the 1950s.

A new multiplicity of television channels in the 1990s raises new problems for sports administrators. In charge of play activities which have always tended to be traditionalist, conservative, and cautious in their attitude to change, they have to relate to a powerful, dynamic medium which has become central to most people's leisure. They face, for instance, the temptation of a high bid from a minority channel which may warm the sport's coffers but then runs the risk of having it under-reported or even ignored by the channels with larger audiences, to the detriment of live support for the competition as a whole. This may well have already begun with the surrender of Sunday afternoon cricket to Sky Television in the 1990 season. Apart from the other effects of television on sport - its treatment of it as entertainment, as staged drama, its focus on action, conflict, and personality - there is the increasing inter-relationship between television and the popular press. Tabloid dailies are, in anyone unacquainted with the latest offerings on the television screen, particularly so far as pop and sport are concerned. They both pick up the same themes, and both, in Britain, have another penchant - the build-up of the star performer followed by his knock-down. It is the reduction of the old classical concept of *hubris* from tragedy to farce.

It is as well to remember, though, that the role of the media in sport is only novel in its intensity. Press coverage of sport began in the eighteenth century and there were regular sporting journals and newspapers by its end. Nineteenth-century newspapers gave sport its own voice and it was a voice which could influence, as well as merely report. The concepts of 'test' matches, and of a county championship were created by the press before they were taken up by the authorities, while newspaper sponsorship of athletics, cycling, bowls, and local football all encouraged the shaping of the sporting scene.

Great as it was, the power of the press then was as nothing compared with the power of television today. Sheer numbers can amaze - there were 8,000 media employees, the majority to do with TV, at the Los Angeles Olympics, more than at any previous event in the world's history. Television is now able to reshape sport to its own ends. In Britain, Rugby league apart the extent to which it has already done so is minimal, but the writing is on the wall. The half-time break in live television soccer is extended to allow for two advertising slots, and the televised Sunday afternoon cricket match is brought forward so as not to run too far into the evening schedules. However, dire warnings come from North America, with its tendency to initiate modern social and sporting fashions. Its own football code has been readily corralled into the best shape for numerous advertising breaks, baseball somewhat less comfortably, though starting times have been arranged for the widest national viewing - the 1990 World Series games in Cincinatti were timed for 8.00 pm local time, which meant that play scarcely started before 8.30, by which time an icy October wind could blow in from the Ohio River. What a way for a summer game to reach its climax! Some encouragement might be taken though, from the experience of soccer's World Cup in the United States in 1994 where the game managed to survive relatively intact despite it not being a friendly game for American advertisers. Apart from half-time, the breaks in play may be there, but they are unpredictable. The pressure for a game of four quarters rather than two halves was successfully resisted and referees still only had to follow signals from television directors at the start of each half.

Overall however the omens are not auspicious. The control by the media, ultimately the control of sport by money the sources of which are not primarily interested in the play itself, must threaten the very nature of modern play. Television has already shown, through Kerry Packer, that if the sports administrators do not pander to the demands of the camera, then powerful companies are quite capable of taking the sport away from them. From the other side, there are already examples of the sacrifice of principle to purse, notably in the award of the 1996 Olympics to Atlanta so soon after the USA's previous games. To save sport for sport, to preserve it as genuine contest, and to preserve it from the circus fate of professional wrestling, will demand from the world's sports organisers a combination of integrity, wisdom, and realistic bargaining, so that their events are served yet not moulded by television and the press. They are qualities which will have to be learned very quickly.

Commentaries about Sunday sport. Background to the debates on changing the Sunday trading laws.

Britain in a Sporting World

There has been not just a great growth of leisure in later twentieth-century Britain. There has been a change in its shape and nature, which has had widespread sporting implications. The availability of a widening range of options in the use of free time, increased car ownership, and the spread of television, have all served to both modify the role of popular sport and at the same time to extend the horizons of its followers to new sporting experience, and to the whole world beyond these shores.

The immediate post-war mood was one of instant jubilation, overtaken almost at once by relief and weariness. The drain of a long and wasting war and the suspension of serious sporting competition soon showed in international results. Football, by 1947, was reeling from England's unthinkable defeat by Switzerland and Scotland's equal humiliation at the hands of Belgium. Britain won only three events in the 1948 Olympics in London, while on the cricket field the test team could not manage to win over the 1949 New Zealanders, and was comprehensively beaten by the West Indians a year later. The British, less unexpectedly, failed at Wimbledon, while the boxers lost their world titles. Things went from bad to worse. At the Helsinki Olympics, the country had to wait until the very last day for its first gold medal - and then it was won by a horse.

The yearning for the past, the thankfulness at the restoration of first-class sport, at first brought the old crowds. Then the gradual realisation that Britain had fallen behind Europe and South America in football, behind the West Indies in cricket, and behind the rest of the world in virtually every other sport, began to dawn. In football, England's first foray into FIFA's World Cup competition ended in incredible defeat by the United States. This might all have happened a long way away - the competition that year was held in Brazil - but the lesson was driven home by the visit of the superb Hungarian team in 1953. A 6-3 loss at home was followed by an even more catastrophic defeat 7-1 in Budapest the following year, and the long ball play of the English was made to look clumsy, outdated and unskilful against the slick new passing style of the continentals. At club level, ventures into European competition was slightly less calamitous, though when the European Cup was instituted as a knock-out for national champions, the Football League, still inward-looking, advised Chelsea not to enter lest it interfere with their own commitments. The Scottish League champions, Hibernian, did so, and were reputed to have become the richer by £25,000 as a result. Sir Matt Busby resisted the League's pressures the following year and his Manchester United team reached the semi-final. The first British victory in continental competition came with Spurs' victory in the Cup Winners' Cup in 1963, and the first victory in the European Cup itself came from Celtic in 1967. Perhaps surprisingly, given the modest showing of Britain abroad, individual players had already been tempted to sell their talents overseas, first and briefly, in South America, and then, more notably, in Italy. One side effect of this emigration, from the late 1950s onwards, was to give impetus to moves to abolish the maximum wage at home, soon followed by freedom of contract for players.

Meanwhile, the geographical bias of the game in England itself was again changing to follow upon economic shifts. The North was going into steady industrial decline, while the South gradually gained in prosperity. Once depressed rural areas, such as East Anglia and the Welsh Marches, achieved something nearer to economic parity, and Hereford, Shrewsbury, Colchester, Ipswich, and Cambridge United took league football to regions where there had been none at all in pre-war days. The change in balance is well illustrated by comparing the subsequent fates of clubs in the Third Division immediately after the war - five of those from its Southern Section would be in the First Division in the 1990s, but there would be none from the old Northern Section. Newcomers to league status, such as Oxford United, Wimbledon, and Ipswich, have won great distinction, though they have usually tended to find it easier to achieve than to maintain. Another geographical change has reversed the drift of the best players from Scotland to England, as old as the game itself. Wealthy Scottish clubs, and particularly Glasgow Rangers, found that they could attract outstanding English players across the border with a virtual guarantee of European competition every year, an opportunity denied to them at home by the exclusion of English clubs from Europe.

The exclusion of English clubs from Europe was a direct result of the Heysel Stadium disaster, at the end of a period in which British clubs had scored great success in all three European cup competitions. Success, though, had come at a price. Groups of British supporters had become the scourge of European football grounds for their rowdyism, aggression, and often violent behaviour. Paradoxically, the ban came at a time when many continental crowds were at least rivalling and often surpassing the disorder of the British, if, as yet, without such consequences as those at Brussels. After the European club ban was lifted the home clubs faced new impediments, the first a consequence of the separate recognition of all four national associations. Their separate international recognition, once a favour, can now be a serious handicap in the European competitions with new limits on the number of non-national players. The leading British teams, and the English clubs in particular, have always looked upon the whole of the British Isles as their province. Liverpool and Manchester United, for instance, in the early 1990s, were always likely to find their English-born players in a distinct minority. This problem was solved by the European Union's employment regulations with their free movement across its frontiers, but the long absence from European competition, and despite Arsenal's success in the Cup-Winners Cup, had left British teams with some years of catching up to do. Nationally, all the home countries have achieved success at some time. Scotland has regularly qualified for the final stages of international competitions, even if they do not always do their game justice once there. Northern Ireland's spasmodic triumphs have been more frequent than the province's limited resources would lead any but an Ulsterman to expect, while in the other Ireland, Jack Charlton's diligent scrutiny of family trees coupled with pragmatic coaching has produced a national team always capable of taking on the best in the world. Much the same approach on the field had taken England to their one World Cup victory, on home soil, in 1966. Since then the country's fortunes have hung fire - never far below the strongest national sides, but with a persistent tendency to disappoint. Reaching the semi-final of the World Cup in Italia 90 was looked upon with some pride, as it was beyond expectations. Just as important, perhaps, was winning the 'Fair Play' award, in a competition where some of the tackling reached new heights of cynicism, and the agonised, if short-lived writhing of some of the tackled reached new heights of histrionics.

The outstanding features of the Union game have been the dominance of a whole sequence of Welsh teams at home, and the sustained superiority of teams from the southern hemisphere on the world stage. The decline in Welsh fortunes at the end of the 1980s coincided with another of the waves of recruitment to Rugby League, taking away some of the country's best talent and the rise of a strong England team under Will Carling's leadership. The wealth coming into the game, particularly from television contracts, and the inability of players to profit at all directly from their rugby fame, produced an early relaxation in the amateur rules in all countries apart from England, though Twickenham's isolation from the rest of the game could not long persist. As to Rugby League, while the qualities and skills of the game have become much more widely appreciated through national coverage on the screens, it still has only tenuous footholds, so far as actual clubs go, outside its original northern territories, and the British XIIIs are hard put to equal teams from Australia and New Zealand.

English cricket runs an uneven course. In two successive winters it produced one of its worst and one of its best overseas performances. The disasters in Australia in 1990/1 can only be partly accounted for by a nonsensical itinerary, which seemed to have been conjured up by an accountant and a television programmer, without much regard to the cricketers. The apparent ease of air travel has meant that tours, one-day internationals and test matches have all proliferated in recent years, and cricket is increasingly being played not for the live audience but for the television cameras. The one-day games are the exception, but again the fall of the English team at the last hurdle in the 1992 World Cup was to some extent a result of an exhaustive if unblemished tour of New Zealand before the hectic schedule of the competition itself. Subsequent England performances have inspired little confidence in the future of the domestic game. Two possible future scenarios present themselves for the game, neither perhaps as fanciful as they might seem at first sight. The popularity of the one-day game might be accepted, however reluctantly, and county matches become a series of three or four one-day games - as in Major League Baseball - or the three day game is retained with spectators either admitted without charge, to provide some atmosphere for the television cameras, or even paid a fee, as extras in the screened drama. The advent of Durham, the first newcomer in the championship for over half a century, may do something to add more spice to county cricket, but it is hard to believe that it will be enough.

In spite of the thin attendances too often found in both, football and cricket remain the two sports to which most would declare a nominal allegiance. It is impossible to chronicle, in a brief survey, the large number of notable British successes on the world stage in the ever-growing range of competitive sports. Many of these have, over the last half century made their appeals, usually local or occasional, though in athletics and now in golf, where Britain has top players in numbers, a steadier picture of support is emerging. For the rest, the past decades leave a kaleidoscope of passing memories. Tennis retains the golden June glories of Wimbledon - so long as it doesn't rain - but the miserable record of British players makes it an isolated landmark in a sport otherwise largely neglected by popular sentiment, its playing progress hampered by lack of facilities and its residual class associations. Virginia Wade's win in the Jubilee Year did briefly recall the memories of the Coronation, a quarter of a century earlier, when Hillary and Tensing climbed Everest, Gordon Richards won the Derby and Stanley Matthews at last had his cup-winner's medal in the FA Cup Final, and for a moment all stood well with our sporting world. Then in golf there was Jacklin's win in the Open Championship, a foretaste of happier times on the links in the 1980s. In athletics there has been a steady string of great players and performances, from Bannister to Jonathan Edwards and such successful occasions as the 1993 World Championships with its wins for Linford Christie, Sally Gunnell and Colin Jackson. In boxing there was Henry Cooper flooring Muhammad Ali in their first championship clash, and occasional champions outside the coveted heavy-weight class. Again, motor-racing, swimming, cycling, bowls, squash rackets, rowing and a host of other sports have all spasmodically produced their world beaters.

As we look to the end of one century and the start of a new, sport finds itself playing a far more notable role in the world than ever in the past. Sport has become another element in international relations, a means of gaining prestige, or a weapon to be used in diplomacy. As it becomes more important to governments and brings ever-greater rewards to performers, the temptation to seek any means to enhance results sometimes becomes irresistible. The use of aids to enhance performance are as old as competitive sport itself. The old pugs were sometimes accused of having leads in their fists, pedestrians of doping themselves up, or, more often of trying to dope their opponents down. Where now does enhancement of performance by medical means cease to be legitimate? Little debate is raised by surgical repairs or restructuring, or by improvements in diet, which have produced better performing bodies. The live questions concern medication which may improve speed or strength - should it be condemned out of hand, or should bans be limited to what is known to have long-term ill effects? Much of the debate over drugs in sport has so far been conducted emotively, at a fairly superficial level, with efforts going into drug identification and policing. Both the resolution of the ethical conflicts, and then the implementation of that resolution will be a major issue for the coming decades.

The future of British sport shares the world's problems over drug-taking, but happily, it appears, on a minor scale. In this respect, it mirrors the nation's role in international sport as a whole - an honourable part, but not, for the most part, one of leadership, in spite of some recent revivals. It is difficult, though, to be optimistic over the more distant prospect. Investment in sport, in terms of both national determination and financial support, has always been modest and is becoming markedly more so by comparison with the rest of the world. The deficiency takes many forms, not all of them blameworthy, such as the ingrained preference for playing rather than training. However, if the strangling of local authority finances from the 1980s continues, so will the run-down of support for numerous leisure and recreational facilities, which will particularly damage those projects which have helped to bring forward sportsmen and sportswomen from the ethnic minorities and less advantaged social backgrounds.

As for the playing and watching of sport at more everyday levels, there is a marked and continuing tendency to diversification, and with it probably

Signs of the Past - street names. The town of Bendigo, Australia, was named after the early Victorian boxer, William Thompson, known always as 'Bendigo'

Public Houses - The Pecking Mill, possibly a cock-fighting venue, and The Starting Post, spurious in one sense, since the King's Arms at Dorchester, of which it forms part, usually celebrated the end rather the start of its races by housing the race ball.

dilution, in the nation's sporting experience. Quite apart from the spread of such sports as bowls, snooker, aerobics, wind-surfing, scuba-diving, winter sports - the list could be almost endless - there is the television interest in once strange sports from across the world. American football, Australian rules, and even sumo wrestling, will undoubtedly be followed by other such as baseball as the new satellite channels seek to fill their viewing time. World or continental leagues will doubtless soon be with us in any number of sports. In soccer it will probably mean that the uneconomic mass of British lower division clubs will decline, gracefully or otherwise, possibly into part-time professionalism. Already, and largely as a result of successful promotion by European television, American football has launched an international league with teams from both sides of the Atlantic, a road likely to be trod by many other competitive sports. It implies that future attempts to analyse sporting activity will have to find some other classification than through nation states. That, if so, will surely be a sign of international sporting health.

The Present and the Past
The present is always on the point of becoming the past - a truism certainly, but it is one with many implications. It makes recent and contemporary history the hardest to write, since we are denied the privilege of standing back and having any long perspective. Fortunately, at least one historian has taken up the challenge - Tony Mason, *Sport in Britain* (London and Boston, 1988) is an excellent and compact review of selected present-day issues in their historical context. Sometimes, too, our own times and our own experiences

are best illuminated by comparison and contrast, and with this in mind Paul Gardner, *Nice Guys Finish Last: Sport and American Life* (London, 1974) presents some fascinating challenges.

Sports history, like any other, is being made every minute and it is important that is should not be lost. The records of major contests are unlikely to vanish, but the memories of much other sport have always been fragile. This, then, is a plea to the thousands of secretaries, treasurers, and other officials of sports clubs of every sort, from the pub darts team to the mountaineering hut, to keep as full accounts as possible of their activities, and to keep those records secure. It is particularly important that, in the event of a club's demise, its records should not disappear with it, but be deposited in some safe place - with the sport's national body, a museum, or a record office. The pictorial records of sport, too, need to be created and preserved. Conventional newspaper pictures seldom tell the full story, and a critical eye behind a camera lens can preserve what otherwise might be lost. This alertness is particularly called for where development is taking place, and old sporting signs, landmarks and facilities from the past are being swept away. Anything other than some major structure such as a football stadium, is unlikely to be much noticed by others.

Sport history, though, is not merely a matter for club officials and keen photographers. It is a topic which can cater for numerous interests. Enthusiasm for a particular sport or a particular team is one of its most obvious starting points, but other beginnings may well be from outside sport itself, particularly as its boundaries become constantly wider. Sportswear, for instance, has now become a significant and fashionable sector of the clothing industry and sporting dress past and present, male and female, offers much scope for the collection of material. The possibilities of heraldry have already been mentioned, given the continuing appearance of heraldic devices in the badges of clubs and other sporting bodies. The geography of sport is virtually at its beginnings and there is endless opportunity to enquire into the distribution of sports and players, both nationally and regionally, while geographers are well equipped to spot the impact of play on landscape - the promoting of the conversion of farm land into leisure facilities is bound to offer much evidence of this. Transport buffs have endless opportunities to run their enthusiasms to sport - we have a fair general picture of the impact of railways in the nineteenth and twentieth centuries, but many local studies to fill out the detail, and possibly adjust the overall impressions, would be very valuable. The same information about road and air travel for sport is also needed. Scientists and engineers can apply their expertise to the many aspects of play that are becoming more and more technical, while even those who want to confine their efforts to an armchair in the sitting room can make useful analyses of the television presentation of sport, its changing modes, its varying attention to individual activities, the impact of competition between channels, and so on. And anyone could keep a sporting diary, or even record interesting sporting events in an ordinary diary - the reactions of people other than players and reporters are always interesting to future researchers, and many nuggets of information have come from the journals of people who had no particularly strong interest in sport as such - Pepys and Evelyn being prime cases - but there are many humbler examples (the bulk of them, incidentally, still lying untitled in record offices).

Beyond the present, the future, too, holds the certain promise of issues which have their roots in the sporting past surveyed here. Among them are such diverse questions as the future of apartheid, the law on Sunday behaviour, the legitimacy of means of enhancing sporting performance, the financing of sporting facilities, and the continued internationalisation of competitive play. Some knowledge of the sporting richness of the past can only illuminate the appreciation of an even richer sporting future.

Index